Life with the Lions

Life with the Lions

The Inside Story of the 1977 New Zealand Tour

John Hopkins

Stanley Paul, London

Stanley Paul & Co Ltd
3 Fitzroy Square, London W1P 6JD

An imprint of the Hutchinson Publishing Group

London Melbourne Sydney Auckland Wellington
Johannesburg and agencies throughout the world

First published 1977
© John Hopkins 1977

Photoset in Plantin by Print Origination Ltd, Merseyside

Printed in Great Britain at The Anchor Press Ltd
and bound by Wm Brendon & Son Ltd,
both of Tiptree, Essex

ISBN 0 09 131740 1

To Susi, who now knows more about this tour than any other wife who stayed behind – and perhaps more than she should. With love and thanks.

Contents

The author wishes to thank Adrian Murrell for providing the photographs.

Introduction

When I set out for New Zealand with the British Lions on 10 May, I had no idea what happened on a rugby tour. Fifteen notebooks, twenty-five tapes and one broken typewriter later I sat down and tried to write a book about the tour. I wanted to explain what it was like to be a British Lion for three and a half months 12 000 miles away from home, to describe what went on both on and off the field and to convey a little of what it was like for me, for them, and for their wives.

If I have failed to do justice to any player, and I am sure I have, then I can only apologize and offer, as a feeble excuse, the demands of an unrelenting publishing schedule.

I feel privileged to have spent fourteen and a half weeks with men I admire watching a game that I love – at someone else's expense. The world is not such a bad place, after all.

London
26 September 1977

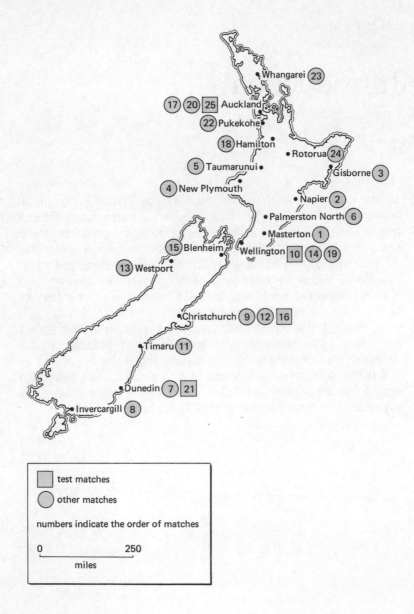

Whangarei (23)

(17) (20) (25) Auckland

(22) Pukekohe

(18) Hamilton

(5) Taumarunui

(4) New Plymouth

•Rotorua (24)

Gisborne (3)

•Napier (2)

•Palmerston North (6)

•Masterton (1)

(15) Blenheim

Wellington (10) (14) (19)

(13) Westport

•Christchurch (9) (12) (16)

•Timaru (11)

•Dunedin (7) (21)

•Invercargill (8)

test matches

other matches

numbers indicate the order of matches

0   250

miles

Chapter 1

Tour or crusade?

A major rugby tour by the British Isles to New Zealand is a cross between a medieval crusade and a prep-school outing. It is one hundred and one days in a foreign country where too many days are the same. For most participants it is too long, too expensive, unnatural and often misunderstood by the people back home. The Lions might be envied by their male friends left behind for being given the freedom of youth once again, an opportunity to escape their mortgages, their bank managers and their mothers-in-law. Most of all for being given the chance to revel in a rugby tour's traditional delights – birds, booze, and being with the boys. But a rugby tour is not a beer-drinking, roll-throwing, fourteen-week Roman orgy. A major tour is both business and pleasure, war and peace.

It is one thousand people asking, 'How do you like our country?' and, 'How are you enjoying yourself?' It is a whirl of twice-weekly journeys by plane, coach and train to another town, another set of welcoming faces, another hotel room, another room-mate, another game. And at the end of it all, back home again, it is one thousand people asking, 'Did you enjoy the tour?'

In New Zealand the Lions were watched from the time they went training in the morning to the moments when they wanted a quiet beer at night and found the hotel bar packed with heavies they didn't know and didn't want to talk to. The Lions were on the front page, the back page, the inside pages of newspapers. Television showed at least an hour's rugby each week. Test matches were previewed, screened live, replayed and then discussed endlessly. Who said it is only a game?

Scarcely a day passed in New Zealand when the Lions were not ogled, questioned, criticized, applauded. They were paid £3 each day as pocket money, a sum set deliberately low so as not to infringe their amateur status, yet they were exploited as much as any professional team. One firm after another cashed in on the Lions, with team photos, souvenir envelopes, brochures and postage stamps. Not a penny came back to the team. It was the rip-off of 1977.

The Lions were heros and anti-heros. They attracted pretty girls to their parties, big crowds to their games. People gave up their jobs and flew thousands of miles to watch them play. In some places the Lions were cheered and made welcome. At other times they were jeered and spat at. They were recognized in the street, attacked in the newspapers. New Zealand *Truth* newspaper called them 'louts' and 'animals'. The *Sunday News* said they were 'lousy lovers' and had an affidavit from one of the Lions' comely conquests to prove it.

And the pressure got greater and greater. 'Now you've beaten us, for God's sake make sure you beat Otago,' they told the Lions in Manawatu. In Canterbury it was, 'Now you've beaten us, for God's sake don't lose to Wellington.' Time and again New Zealanders would say, 'May the best team win – so long as it is ours.'

So why did the Lions do it? As amateurs they had a perfect right to say no to it all, and some players did. No other amateur sport inflicts on its players and their families such a long and demanding tour. Once the tour started there was no escape. Their passports were taken away from them in London and not returned until the end of the tour. Despite this, to be chosen as a Lion is the crown and the glory. Fran Cotton went to New Zealand because it gave him a sense of fulfilment. 'Now I have been a Lion in South Africa and New Zealand I have done it all,' says the rugged Englishman. Andy Irvine, the Scottish full back, says, 'Once you've toured New Zealand as a Lion no one can ever take that away from you, even if you have had a terrible tour.'

As he spoke Irvine was bustling around his hotel room, sealing a parcel he was sending back to his home in Edinburgh. It contained programmes and some presents he had bought. He had been a Lion in South Africa in 1974. Had there been more presents for the players, frees they call them, this time? 'Nothing like,' he replied, though he was not complaining. 'This is almost the only thing we have been given.' He held up a silver tray he and all the Lions had received from the Auckland union. 'In South Africa we were given tankards, wallets, a sheepskin even, and a tie almost everywhere. In fact, you were soon almost sick of ties. The South African Rugby Union gave us each two Springboks. Generally they were a lot more generous.'

Being a Lion is an odd experience. In New Zealand the players were participating in the national game and therefore they received much more respect than they would at home. On the other hand, being on tour was like being on a school outing. Every conceivable thing was done for them.

There was one man who handled their baggage, sewed on their buttons, massaged their aches and pains. Another answered their mail. At each of eighteen towns and cities the Lions visited in New Zealand, golf clubs opened their doors, and snooker and pool tables were always available somewhere. A local rugby union official was briefed to arrange other excursions: jet boating in flat-bottom boats up a local river, deep-sea fishing, free cinema tickets, free entry to a local race meeting. The better liaison men supplied good tips as well.

An injured Lion gets the best available medical advice, being whisked to and from the hospital by car or taxi, all paid for by the New Zealand Rugby Union. But oddly, a fit Lion does not always stay in the best hotels. Fit or sick though, Lions always share rooms, and their rooms are a jumble of boots and bags and clothes. Only the captain, manager and coach do not have to share rooms.

A Lion is told what to do from the time the bus leaves for training in the morning, which uniform he must wear to the party in the evening, and how much and what he can drink at dinner. For some, like Mike Gibson, who was on his fifth Lions tour, it was a sort of holiday. He finds that being organized by others is no more disturbing to him, as a successful solicitor used to organizing his own life, than is any change of routine. 'I have my routine at home,' says Gibson. 'And I have my routine on tour. Playing rugby on tour is like going to the office back home. It is all a matter of self-discipline.'

And sometimes a Lion is told what not to do. He must not

drink wine with his meal except on certain days and then only New Zealand wine. He can send out his laundry and dry cleaning as often as he likes but he cannot make a phone call unless he pays for it himself. In many hotels the Lions ate only table d'hôte and drank only soft drinks with their meals.

A Lion has to sign a thousand autographs – more if he is Andy Irvine, the pin-up boy of the tour – visit schools and hospitals, field enquiring telephone calls, friendly and abusive, at any time of the day or night. He must mind his *P*s and *Q*s and always say, 'Please' and, 'Thank you.'

Ripping open an envelope in Christchurch, Mike Gibson found a one-dollar note and a brief letter: 'Please can I have a Lions jersey?'

As the tour ended I asked Ian McGeechan what it had been like to be a 1977 Lion. He hardly needed to say a great deal, for his appearance told it all. He looked pale and exhausted and he spoke like the tired man he undoubtedly was. 'It has been very difficult, probably more difficult than being a 1971 or 1974 Lion because we had to carry a mantle that they did not. We had to come back and try and achieve something for a second time.

'It has been a great honour being a Lion but if people back home think we have had a holiday out here then I'll be putting a few of them straight when I get back. I reckon everybody on this tour party has paid in full for the honour they were given purely for the pressure they have had to undergo.'

From the time they left London on 10 May until their return on 19 August the Lions made 30 separate flights, 10 major coach trips and 1 train ride. They took off and landed 70 times from 20 different airports on 3 continents. They had travelled in all nearly 40 000 miles, played 26 games of rugby, been watched by 718 000 spectators (and millions more on television) and earned the New Zealand rugby union £1 191 000 (NZ$2 025 000) in gate takings from the 25 games in New Zealand.

As they set out on their crusade that warm spring day in May few of them realized what lay ahead of them. New Zealand was about to become their Holy Land.

Chapter 2

Who's in, who's out, and who couldn't make it

To wear the red jersey, white shorts, and blue-and-green stockings of the British Isles rugby-union touring team, the British Lions, is the highest honour that can be given to a player from England, Scotland, Wales and Ireland. Since the first British Isles team visited Australia and New Zealand in 1888 a further eight have left for tours of either Australia or New Zealand or both. The 1977 Lions, then, were the tenth in ninety years.

Until 1971 the Lions were regularly beaten by the hardy farmers who dominated New Zealand teams. Then in 1971 a magnificently talented team that included Gareth Edwards and Barry John at half back, the great Irish centre Mike Gibson, full back J.P.R. Williams and the tall slender No. 8 Mervyn Davies, ended this doleful record. They won the Test series 2–1, with one match drawn.

Three years later the Lions toured South Africa, and whether up on the veldt or down at sea level they proved invincible. Basing their tactics around one of the finest forward packs ever to play for Britain, the Lions won twenty-one of their twenty-two matches, drawing the fourth and final Test, 13–13. Britain were now the world champions.

Nothing less than complete success was expected from the 1977 team. The excitement around Britain was great as the time for team selection grew near. Who would be picked? In Wales it became almost a national issue as they argued in clubs and pubs.

There had been thirteen Welshmen in 1971 but only nine in South Africa. How many would there be this time? Wales won the Grand Slam in 1975/6 and the Triple Crown in 1976/7, and under the guidance of John Dawes had lost only two matches in three seasons.

After an illustrious playing career which reached its peak when he captained the victorious Lions in 1971, Dawes had become Britain's outstanding coach. He was the natural choice to mastermind the 1977 team. As manager, the four Home Unions tours committee selected George Burrell, a 57-year-old former Scottish international and top-class referee, who had successfully managed a short tour of New Zealand by Scotland in 1975.

But the third appointment in the trio, that of the captain, was a more difficult one to make. There was Roger Uttley, the craggy English forward from Gosforth, who was soon to captain England. And there was Phil Bennett from Llanelli, the most brilliant stand off in rugby. Yet there were doubts about both of them: Uttley suffered from an unusual back injury, which in the end was to prevent him going on the tour. And Bennett, who had been desperately homesick when he was with the Lions in South Africa three years ago, didn't really want to leave his family again for so long.

In the autumn of 1976 Pat, Phil Bennett's wife, looked happy and contented. Bennett's job with Courage, the brewers, was going well and their little son Steven had just begun to take his first tottering steps. On his 28th birthday on 24 October 1976, Phil thought that the world could scarcely be a more pleasant place.

He didn't really want to take part in another Lions tour. He had been disappointed at not being picked to tour New Zealand in 1971 but he had had a pleasant summer playing cricket. He and Pat were married that summer and went for a brief honeymoon in North Wales. He had enjoyed being a British Lion in South Africa in 1974 but when he came back he felt that one Lions tour was enough.

When people started asking him about the 1977 tour to New Zealand his answer was ready. 'I'm not going, I'm not available. I don't think it's fair on my wife and child. Steven is getting to the age where I have to sneak out of the house each morning so he doesn't see or hear me go.' Bennett even wrote to the management of the tour and said that he wasn't available.

In February 1977 he remarked to a friend, 'Why should I go

to New Zealand for four months when the most important thing in the world to me is coming home each evening and seeing my wife and little son?'

Bennett was not alone in turning down the forthcoming tour. At least four leading players had declared themselves unavailable for the gruelling 14½-week journey: Englishman Peter Dixon, and Welshmen J.P.R. Williams, Gerald Davies and Gareth Edwards. Mervyn Davies, the great No. 8, revealed later that he too would have been unavailable had he not been forced to give up rugby after a brain haemorrhage in 1976.

It could not have been entirely coincidental that all of them had been to New Zealand before. Dixon, Gerald and Mervyn Davies, Williams and Edwards with the 1971 Lions; Bennett as a precocious 20-year-old with Wales on the disastrous short tour in May and June 1969.

There were various reasons for their unavailability, the main one being work. This was only natural for men in their late twenties and early thirties who were building successful careers and felt they had to put work ahead of rugby.

Peter Dixon, a lecturer at Durham University, had to stay and mark exam papers on African social anthropology. Dr J.P.R. Williams, a rising doctor at the massive University Hospital of Wales, Cardiff, was in line for a job as a registrar and had to stay behind for an interview. Gareth Edwards, 29, and Gerald Davies, 32, were simply too busy at work. All of them undoubtedly felt that after being so successful in New Zealand six years earlier some of the incentive had gone. They knew, too, that whereas tours of South Africa had some easy matches where the Lions could be expected to win by seventy or eighty points, in New Zealand life would be harder. There would be no easy games.

Another factor may have been that all of them were now married and most had children. To ask participants in an amateur sport to leave their wives and children for a 36 000-mile trip around the world spread over fourteen weeks at some considerable financial cost to themselves was an outdated and unrealistic request and one out of keeping with the 1970s, the decade of women's liberation. Rugby takes up more time than it used to; yet in some ways, it is accorded less importance in the life of players today than it once was. The maximum length tour the players would have considered would have been fifteen matches, including three Tests, spread over eight or nine weeks.

Even for journalists the trip wasn't necessarily going to be fourteen weeks in paradise. I viewed the touring with mixed feelings. The last time I was asked if I was looking forward to the trip I remembered the words that W.C. Fields has on his gravestone: 'On the whole I'd rather be in Philadelphia,' and I said that I hoped when I returned I wouldn't be saying something similar.

Still, I had to go, and in his heart of hearts Phil Bennett knew he had to go too. Towards the end of 1976 he began to have doubts about his decision not to be available. They came slowly and privately at first.

Then he was appointed captain of Wales and, far from being nervous about it as the Phil Bennett of a few years earlier would have been, he grew in confidence. 'I looked at it like this,' he recalled one day. 'At the time I was asked to captain Wales I was already leading the backs and calling the moves. So I thought to myself, I may as well take over the whole team, and to tell you the truth now, I like it.'

His wife Pat, sensing her husband's growing confidence, began to encourage him. 'You've got to go to New Zealand now,' she would say and deep down Bennett wanted to. He felt that had he pulled out of the tour he would have been disappointed with himself. And in years to come his son Steven, for whom he was almost prepared to give up the tour, would be proud of his father. 'Look Phil,' Syd Millar, coach of the 1974 Lions, said to him one day, 'my sons were the same age as yours when I went on the Lions tour but now they look back with pride on what I achieved.'

The scales were finally tipped by the subtle handling by John Dawes, who knew Bennett particularly well, and by Lions manager George Burrell. 'George spoke to me several times but he never once said, "You've got to come." He just said, "We would like you to come. We think it could be a good tour." And I appreciated this kind of approach.'

Week after week in the early part of 1977 Dawes and Bennett put off a serious conversation about New Zealand. When they finally sat down Phil's mind was made up anyway.

'That's it. I'm going,' he had said to himself a few days earlier, telling only Pat about his decision. Any doubts were dispelled after the Wales *v* England game at Cardiff when George Burrell went up to Bennett and said, 'Glad to know you're coming, Benny.'

'Before I had time to say anything,' recalls Bennett, 'George had scarpered off. I told them I was available immediately after that game and confirmed it in a phone call to John Dawes a few days later.' Dawes was pleased as he wanted Bennett to be captain. What remained was the selection of the team.

By the first post on Thursday 24 March, the announcement was received in the offices of the Press Association and Exchange Telegraph in London to be released to newspapers, radio and television throughout Britain and the rest of the world. The thirty players who had been chosen to tour New Zealand were:

1	P. Bennett (Capt.)	*Llanelli and Wales*
2	J.D. Bevan	*Aberavon and Wales*
3	G.L. Brown	*West of Scotland and Scotland*
4	D. Burcher	*Newport and Wales*
5	T.J. Cobner	*Pontypool and Wales*
6	F.E. Cotton	*Sale and England*
7	W.P. Duggan	*Blackrock College and Ireland*
8	Gareth L. Evans	*Newport and Wales*
9	T.P. Evans	*Swansea and Wales*
10	S.P. Fenwick	*Bridgend and Wales*
11	C.M.H. Gibson	*NIFC and Ireland*
12	B.H. Hay	*Boroughmuir and Scotland*
13	N.E. Horton	*Moseley and England*
14	A.R. Irvine	*Heriot's FP and Scotland*
15	A.J. Martin	*Aberavon and Wales*
16	I.R. McGeechan	*Headingley and Scotland*
17	D.W. Morgan	*Stewart's-Melville FP and Scotland*
18	A. Neary	*Broughton Park and England*
19	P.A. Orr	*Old Wesley and Ireland*
20	G. Price	*Pontypool and Wales*
21	D.L. Quinnell	*Llanelli and Wales*
22	H. Elgan Rees	*Neath*
23	P.J. Squires	*Harrogate and England*
24	R.M. Uttley	*Gosforth and England*
25	G.A.D. Wheel	*Swansea and Wales*
26	P.J. Wheeler	*Leicester and England*

27	Clive Williams	*Aberavon and Wales*
28	D.B. Williams	*Cardiff*
29	J.J. Williams	*Llanelli and Wales*
30	R.W. Windsor	*Pontypool and Wales*

It was signed by A.E. Agar, Hon. Secretary of the Four Home Rugby Unions' Tours Committee, the body of Irish, Scots, Welsh and Englishmen who organized overseas tours by the Lions and tours to Britain and Ireland by visiting countries. The announcement was dated 23 March 1977.

The team comprised sixteen Welshmen, the largest number from any one country to be selected for a Lions tour in modern times, six Englishmen, of whom five were forwards, five Scots, of whom four were backs, and three Irishmen. Geoff Wheel, the Swansea forward, dropped out of the team the week they were due to gather in London on medical advice and was replaced by Irishman Moss Keane.

No one had anticipated that the four selectors and the chairman George Burrell would select so many Welshmen once J.P.R. Williams, Gareth Edwards and Gerald Davies declined to be considered for the tour. This was the doing of coach John Dawes, who although not officially a selector had a very influential voice in the composition of the team.

The speedy Scots centre, Jim Renwick, was surprisingly not picked, nor was the Scottish loose head prop Ian McLauchlan, who it was thought could contribute much to scrummaging technique even though he was 35.

Scot Bruce Hay might not have got the second full back position had Englishman Alastair Hignell been available, but he was not because of exams at Cambridge University. A talented all-rounder, Hignell was also captain of the University at cricket.

Gareth Evans was a name new to many outside Wales. The 24-year-old Newport player, a representative with a finance company, had come on as a replacement for Gerald Davies in the game against France in February and fifteen minutes was the extent of his international experience.

Clive Williams, one of the loose head props, had only been picked for Wales last season as a replacement when Charlie Faulkner was injured and he played in the last two games of the championship.

There were two uncapped players in the party: Brynmor Williams, the scrum half whose selection had long been anticipated once Gareth Edwards, the man he had understudied at Cardiff, was not available, and winger Elgan Rees of Neath. Both went on to join the select band capped by the British Isles before their country. The stocky, fast Elgan Rees would certainly have played for Wales on the right wing in 1976/7 but for the continued presence of the outstanding Gerald Davies.

It was a feature of the three quarters as announced that many could play in different positions. Gareth Evans could play centre or wing, though he was picked as a wing; Andy Irvine could come forward from full back to the right wing; Ian McGeechan could play centre, stand off or, as he proved in the third Test, wing; and Mike Gibson stand off or centre. Phil Bennett played for Llanelli the previous season on the wing and then represented the Lions on the left wing against the Bay of Plenty and Fiji at the end of the tour.

This versatility extended to the forwards too. Roger Uttley, later to drop out because of his back injury, could play second row, blind side flanker or No. 8, as could Derek Quinnell. Tony Neary had played No. 8 for Lancashire as well as flanker. Fran Cotton could play both tight and loose head prop, and hooker Bobby Windsor was able to play tight head prop as well.

The announcement of the team was embargoed until mid-day in Britain on Thursday and eleven in the evening in New Zealand. The tour was on but it took a while for some of the players to hear the good news.

At one o'clock that same Thursday Scotsman Gordon Brown was 30 000 feet above the Atlantic flying to Bermuda to play rugby in a festival. The big lock was desperate to hear the Lions team which he knew would be announced about mid-day. He had been a Lion in 1971 and 1974 and would have been a certainty for this particular tour had he not been suspended for most of the international season. How could he hear the team? Six months earlier he had sold his house in Troon to an air traffic controller at Prestwick airport.

Before leaving for Bermuda, Brown, 28, asked the man to listen to the news and radio the pilot of Brown's plane if the Scotsman had been picked. 'About ten past one the pilot came down the aisle and when he picked me out he congratulated me.

I was over the moon as you can imagine and then the celebrations began.'

Down in Wales, Clive Williams only had one reason for rushing home for lunch that Thursday and that was to see how his wife Jenny was feeling. She was expecting their first child at any time. Clive had hardly got through the front door of their home in Porthcawl, South Wales, before Jenny had thrust an envelope in front of him. It was the notification of his selection for the Lions. 'I think the excitement of it put the wife's blood pressure up and I had to rush her into hospital,' recalls Williams, 27. The following Saturday Williams was in the Aberavon team that was defeated by Cardiff in a semi-final of the Welsh Cup. After the game he went to Neath Hospital and in the early hours of Sunday morning his wife gave birth to a little girl they named Tracy.

Moss Keane was out of his office in Dublin the morning that Albert Agar rang; when he returned he found Agar's message and one from Ronnie Dawson waiting for him. He had heard that Welshman Geoff Wheel was out of the tour on medical grounds and so he suspected what the calls were about. The big Irish lock rang Ronnie Dawson who told him he was selected. 'You start trying to get permission to leave work,' said Dawson. 'I'll start at the top and you start at the bottom and we'll meet halfway.' Ten minutes later Keane had got permission from the Department of Agriculture. Then he called Albert Agar in London.

'You're in the team,' said Agar, expecting Keane to be excited.

'Oh yes,' said Moss, enjoying his private joke enormously. 'What else is new?'

Chapter 3

Getting together

The Lions were on the move. Their orders were to meet at The Star and Garter hotel in Richmond, London, by 4.30 p.m. on Friday 6 May. The three from Edinburgh, Andy Irvine, Douglas Morgan and Bruce Hay, and manager George Burrell, who lived in Galashiels, flew to Gatwick in the morning. Burrell was whisked to London in a BBC car to give an interview. From Wales Phil Bennett came up by train an hour or so before Derek Quinnell, John Bevan, Elgan Rees, Allan Martin and J.J. Williams, who all lived near each other in the Port Talbot, Porthcawl area of South Wales, caught a mid-morning train and arrived at Paddington just after lunch.

Irishmen Mike Gibson from Belfast and Willie Duggan and Phil Orr from Dublin, together with Moss Keane, flew over on Friday morning. Englishman Roger Uttley came from his small village outside Newcastle. He had left home soon after seven for he was to attend a lunch in London starting at noon.

As the players made their way to London from all points of the compass a flurry of activity started behind them. Many wives didn't want to spend three and a half months on their own and had arranged to move to relatives or to have friends come and stay. Andy Irvine's wife Audrey was expecting her first baby in July and was leaving their new home to move to her mother's in Northern Ireland. J.J. Williams's wife Janey, who was expecting a baby in October, was planning to move in with her friend Janet Martin, the wife of Allan, in Port Talbot. At week-ends Wendy Fenwick, Steve's wife, would visit as would Marleen Evans, Trevor's wife, and Elgan Rees's wife of eight months, Kathryn.

'I'm scared to death of being alone in a house,' said Kathryn. She was joined by an old school friend, her parents and other relatives at various times.

Anne, Brenda and Judy, the wives of the three Pontypool players Graham Price, Terry Cobner and Bobby Windsor, were planning to meet once each week for a drink and a chat, and they expected David Burcher's wife Margaret and Gareth Evans's girl-friend to join them as often as possible. 'My Mum lives over the road anyway and Bobby's is only ten minutes away,' said Judy Windsor. 'I've got no parents and Graham's Mum will come and lodge,' said Anne Price.

An exception was Pat Bennett, the wife of the Lions' captain. She had thought of taking her son Steven to stay with her parents in Swiss Valley just five minutes away by car but decided against it in the end. 'Here we have no nice back garden,' said Pat, waving her hand towards the back of her house in Felinfoel. 'If we go to my parents for three months where it is so nice with green fields and all then I'd never get Steven back here again. So my sister Tracy, who is taking her O-levels this summer, will come and live in, and my mother and Phil's mother will pop in all the time, too.'

Being left alone is a fate that the wives of top rugby players have become accustomed to as the growth of rugby makes tours more frequent. Scotland went to New Zealand for five weeks in 1975 and Ireland went there the following summer. Wales toured Japan in September 1975 and will go to Fiji and Australia in 1978. Of the four home countries, only England have not been on tour since the Lions went to South Africa in 1974.

Rugby wives are closely involved in the game and understand the demands it makes on players, even if they are not entirely happy about it. Anne Price's grandfather, for example, had been the trainer of Pontypool where she met Graham. 'Even if I played for Newport she would still be at Pontypool each week,' says Graham.

But understanding doesn't make it any easier to say goodbye. 'Madora was brought up with brothers who went touring,' explains Derek Quinnell. 'Her brother Alan [Barry John's brother] went to Argentina and then Barry was always going all over the place. But she likes to say goodbye from about 400 yards and from behind a concrete post, half-looking and trying not to cry. Mind you I'm not much good at it either. I was watching *Roots* on television the other night and there was this guy saying goodbye to his wife and children. All of a sudden I thought to myself, "I don't want to go to New Zealand."' Quinnell screwed up his eyes and pretended to cry. 'The consolation was that he was going for fourteen years and I was only going for fourteen weeks.'

Janet Martin was particularly worried. She was due to have her second child in July. When giving birth to her first in the summer of 1974 she had had a brain haemorrhage and had still not recovered. 'I want Allan to go but I want him to be here with me too,' she said before the tour began. Right up to the end Martin would have dropped out had his wife's resolve weakened, but it was she who had insisted at the start that he should go and she maintained it to the end.

Two days before the Lions were due to gather in London Ian McGeechan moved into a brand-new house in Leeds. He had time only to look around before leaving it. His wife was in charge of the settling in. The same day Douglas Morgan's wife Doreen had a miscarriage with what would have been their second child but like Janet Morgan she was determined that her husband should go on the tour. On Friday both men travelled down to London.

The Lions were leaving for this long tour virtually unpaid, save for a small daily allowance of pocket money which would not be enough for anything more than the most modest needs. This meant that any player who had to take unpaid leave from his employer would be considerably out of pocket by the time he returned in mid August. Most players thought they would need £200 of their own money for presents, entertaining friends, phone calls home and the dozens of postcards they were expected to send.

Most of the Lions were paid their normal salary by their employers while they were away. The Welsh education authorities had no political objections to the Lions touring New Zealand and so gladly approved paid leaves of absence for teachers John Bevan, Allan Martin, Elgan Rees, David Burcher, Brynmor Williams, Terry Cobner and, later, Jeff Squire, who replaced Roger Uttley. Their attitude was the same as that of

Ian McGeechan's headmaster. 'He thinks I am doing a good job for the school,' said McGeechan. 'So he is prepared to let me have the necessary time off.'

They were luckier than J.J. Williams, who in 1974 was a physical education teacher. His local education authority decided as a gesture of their disapproval of the Lions going to South Africa that they would not pay Williams while he was away.

Bruce Hay's employers, the National Coal Board, for whom he worked as an electrician at a colliery just outside Edinburgh, were paying him for the length of the tour.

But Clive Williams, a beetle-browed Welshman from Porthcawl, was not so fortunate. He was a plasterer with a local firm; though they had kindly promised he could have his job back when he returned they couldn't pay him while he was away. As he had only been picked for his country against England seven weeks before he had not considered he had any chance of making the tour and so had made no attempt to save money. Williams was undoubtedly delighted to become a father just before he left but it did mean his wife was unable to earn any money while he was away and so for fifteen weeks there was virtually no income coming into the house.

Willie Duggan, a genial Irishman with a thick brogue, ran an electrical business with a half dozen employees in Kilkenny, south of Dublin. He was going to lose money by being away as was his countryman Moss Keane, who was forced to use his annual holiday from the Department of Agriculture in Eire to go on tour. When his holiday ended he was on unpaid leave for the remaining ten weeks.

Steve Fenwick had left his teaching position at a large comprehensive in Caerphilly and not yet started his new job as a sales representative so there was a period when he was not earning anything. Luckily, his wife Wendy was able to do some bread-winning as a nurse at an hospital in Cardiff.

Scotsman Doug Morgan was self-employed. He was a chiropodist in Edinburgh with a thriving practice on Princes Street. In a normal day he would see as many as sixteen patients in his surgery and sometimes would spend an evening making house visits as well. He was closing down his practice while he was away except for two days each week when his wife Doreen, a trained chiropodist, could help out. Morgan estimated the Lions tour would cost him £750 in lost income.

For these players, then, the amount of the allowance paid to them became critically important. In 1971 when decimalization was introduced it was changed from fifteen shillings per day to its exact equivalent, 75 pence, and it was announced as if the players had won the pools. The amount remained the same for the Lions in South Africa in 1974 but early in 1977 the International Board decided to raise it to £3 or N Z $ 5.50. Even the most skilful husbandry couldn't make that money last in New Zealand where, for example, a bottle of shampoo cost £1. Accommodation, meals, transport and occasional outings to the cinema were all paid for by their hosts. But the Lions had to pay for their phone calls home, which were to cost them over two dollars each minute.

Rules for the crusade stipulated, among other things, that wives and girl-friends were to be left behind. The Four Home Unions' Tours Committee told players that no facilities 'have been, or can be, made available by the New Zealand R F U for visitors from home to join members of the party or to travel with them at any stage of the tour'. They felt that wives, fiancées and girl-friends could have an unsettling effect on the rest of the players.

Despite this traditional ruling, Moyra Gibson, Mike's wife, flew out to New Zealand for the last five weeks of the tour.

All this was still weeks away as the players made their way down to Richmond. The Star and Garter is a recently modernized hotel on a hill overlooking the Thames, and after the Lions had arrived they set about getting to know each other. Everybody knew John Dawes and Phil Bennett. In the main though, the only players who knew manager George Burrell were the Scots.

He is six foot tall, greying, with glasses and looks younger than 57. He had played full back for Scotland and later became an international referee. He looks to the world as most people imagine a friendly bank manager should and speaks with a thick Scottish accent that some of the players at first couldn't understand. And they kept wondering who 'Dod' was until a Scot pointed out that it was a Border nickname for George.

All in all it was a disparate lot that gathered in London that calm May evening – except for their excellence at and their love for rugby. The average age of the players was 27½. The youngest was 23-year-old Elgan Rees who had never been on tour before and the oldest was Mike Gibson, 11 years older and making his fifth Lions tour. Twenty-two of them were married, six were bachelors and two, Peter Squires and Fran Cotton, were engaged and planning to get married on consecutive days in October. Without knowing of the other's intentions each had even booked a brief honeymoon in the Lake District.

The most common occupation was teaching. There were eleven teachers in all. The others had jobs ranging from Willie Duggan's electrical business to civil engineering, which Graham Price was studying at University in Cardiff. Probably the most qualified Lion was Moss Keane who had a B Sc. in dairy science and then a master's degree in micro-biology.

The first thing that happened after arriving was that they were given a tour number that would be fixed to their luggage and often in the next months would become almost more important than their own names. The numbers were allocated according to the alphabetical order of their surnames so that captain Phil Bennett was number 1 and Bobby Windsor number 30. George Burrell and John Dawes were 31 and 32 and Moss Keane, having replaced Geoff Wheel, became 33. Wheel's number, 25, was left vacant. As soon as the Lions arrived in New Zealand the physiotherapist cum baggage man, Doc Murdoch, joined the party and was given number 34.

The purpose of tour numbers was to enable quick roll calls to be made among the party. If, for example, they were on a bus and wanting to know whether everyone was present someone would shout, 'Give me a number', and one by one the Lions would reply. A missing number meant a missing Lion.

Then the new Lions were introduced to another feature of touring rugby teams. Each day one player would be duty boy. It was the duty boy's job to make sure that everyone knew what was going on that day, what time the coach left for training, what uniform should be worn for any functions there might be, what was happening that evening. He got all this information by seeing the manager each morning straight after breakfast.

In New Zealand the duty boy would hand out the mail, ask all the team members what they wanted to eat for lunch the next day if it was the day of a match, and deliver the food order to the chef. Duty boy would even be responsible for fetching the ice creams when the team went to the cinema. He was in charge of getting all the Lions, including Leo the mascot, on the team coach and off again. Leo was once left behind only momentarily and was kidnapped. Duty boy of the day Billy Beaumont, whose job it was to look after this essential member of the team, was blamed and led an unsuccessful Leo hunt. No ransom was demanded and Leo was never recovered.

Thirdly, Burrell and Dawes explained the committee system to make the day-to-day affairs run smoother on tour. There was to be an inner cabinet of the most senior players representing the four countries to liaise with the management. They met once or twice each week and relayed to George 'what the boys want and what they don't want', explained Bobby Windsor, an inner cabinet member. On the committee with Windsor were Ian McGeechan, Fran Cotton, Mike Gibson and Phil Bennett and, of course, George Burrell and John Dawes.

There was a social committee headed by Tony Neary to organize parties and a committee to distribute free gifts (Bruce Hay and Gareth Evans). J.J. Williams and Allan Martin were responsible for organizing visits by the Lions to hospitals, retired servicemen's association homes and to schools. Derek Quinnell handled the sale of tickets, Peter Wheeler and John Bevan were the bankers. There was even a Postmaster General – Andy Irvine.

The Lions all looked very smart as they arrived at Richmond in a Lions uniform of blue blazer, grey flannels, white shirt and Lions tie. The blazer and flannels had been individually tailored at their local branch of the Simon shops. This was a much better arrangement than in previous years when the outfitting was done in a rush at the assembly point.

They had more formal clothes to take than many Lions teams of recent years. They had two uniforms of blazers and grey flannels, and two Lions ties. One uniform was known as number one and the other as number two. They were basically the same except that the number one blazer was slightly darker and had a smaller, more discreet Lions badge. Instead of a Lions tie a bow tie could be worn with it. Number one rig was for high days and holidays and to be worn on formal occasions such as the British High Commissioner's cocktail party in Wellington. Number two rig, with its larger badge representing the four home countries, was worn on all other occasions.

In addition to their blazers and flannels the Lions were given two white shirts, two casual shirts provided by Adidas, one red polo neck sweater and one blue V-neck sweater complete with the Lions badge, provided by Pringle. To carry their clothes the Lions each had a 22-inch blue hold-all from Adidas, stamped with the initials B I R U T 1977 (British Isles Rugby Union Tour 1977). In addition they had black folding cases, again provided by Adidas, and Air New Zealand gave each of them a handbag-sized travelling bag and an airline bag.

And, of course, they had their private clothes. The official guidance they had before they left, which sounded as though it was written in 1934, said they would need a woollen scarf, a pair of gloves and a small hand towel. But what they really needed were some casual clothes, jeans, some coloured shirts and perhaps a comfortable jacket in case they got tired of wearing their blazer. Any more would simply be unused, unnecessary weight that would cut down the spare space in their cases for their shopping at the end of the tour.

For training in London before they left they had to provide their own practice kit, which was later sent home. For the tour they were given a red Lions track suit, and one white and one red shirt to help when they formed different teams in training. They had to provide their own boots and stockings but an Adidas representative was at the assembly at Richmond to provide them with what they needed. The official sets of Lions jerseys for use in matches – jerseys, shorts and stockings – were provided but kept separate and handled in New Zealand by Doc Murdoch.

The last few days in England were a whirl of medical examinations, training sessions and farewell parties. The whole team had an easy training session followed by a medical at Twickenham on Saturday morning. They watched the Rugby League Cup Final in the afternoon and in the evening attended a dinner given by the Four Home Unions at The East India and Sports Club in St James's Square, where the team had been picked six weeks earlier.

On Sunday morning Roger Uttley aggravated his back injury as he got out of bed and it was decided he should travel back to his home near Newcastle and rest before flying out to New Zealand rather than risk worsening his back on a long flight. His back did not get better and a little over two weeks later Jeff Squire, the Newport and Wales back row forward, flew to New Zealand to take Uttley's place.

The night before they left they were presented with a franking machine by the firm Pitney-Bowes who had donated 300 dollars worth of stamps to the Lions. Andy Irvine was put in charge of it. In thanking Pitney-Bowes and the Rugby Writers' Club for giving the party, manager George Burrell established the pattern he was to follow in New Zealand of telling his statutory dirty joke which was well received by the all-male gathering. He hoped there would be another party to celebrate when the Lions returned.

By Tuesday they were all anxious to get off. Roger Uttley summed up their feelings well: 'I feel dreadful about leaving home but it is a job of work. Let's get on with it.'

Chapter 4

Getting away

Tuesday 10 May was a beautiful day. The sun was warm as it shone from a crystal-clear blue sky. Summer was here. Wearing their number two rig and looking apprehensive the Lions arrived at London airport a little behind schedule. Flight BA 599 to Los Angeles was due to leave at 15.55. They were whisked through customs and on board the Boeing 747 a quarter of an hour ahead of the other passengers.

They installed themselves in the back of the plane and immediately began to change out of their hot blazers and flannels into shorts and casual shirts. A thoughtful stewardess brought in a pile of *Western Mail* newspapers, which carried a special pull out supplement on the Lions, but everybody was too busy undressing to take much notice. After a while a steward checked that they were all decent and then allowed the other passengers on board.

The flight was long but as far as Los Angeles time passed quite quickly. There were not many other passengers and most of the players were able to stretch out. Nigel Horton and Allan Martin commandeered six seats in the middle of the jumbo and slept head to toe.

John Dawes was the noisiest member of the party whether sitting among a group of forwards playing cards or standing in the front bar drinking gin and tonic. In Los Angeles there was forty-five minutes delay before clearing immigration. Reboarding the same plane, we were greeted by stunning stewardesses in long blue and white dresses. The Air New Zealand crew had taken over from British Airways and were to look after us until we reached Auckland.

There was a stop-over in Honolulu and it was pitch dark as we got out of the plane. The big question was: 'What day was it?' Standing in the warm rain Derek Quinnell said firmly, 'I think it's Wednesday.'

'No, it's still Tuesday,' said Moss Keane, who was wearing his airline slippers.

'It's Thursday already,' said someone else.

Quinnell abruptly ended the argument. 'Who cares?' he said. 'What the hell are we doing here getting soaking wet?' and he led the race back onto the plane.

By now the journey was more than half over. Meals came and went, orange juice, eggs, tea or coffee. The films were *Nickelodeon, The Seven Per Cent Solution* and *The Gumball Rally*. The Lions slept through them all.

Flight TE555 landed at Auckland just before eight on Thursday morning 12 May. By 8.30 the Lions' luggage was all neatly piled in one corner of the arrival hall and a coach was ready to take them to a near-by hotel where they lazed for three hours.

At noon they flew down to Wellington, and a small welcoming party including Ces Blazey, chairman of the New Zealand Rugby Union Council, and the NZRFU secretary Jack Jeffs was there to greet them. The Lions had lunch at a local golf club and travelled by coach for two hours to Masterton, where they were to stay for the first week. Within an hour or so of arriving Dawes was in the bar talking to journalists and Phil Bennett, Moss Keane and Mike Gibson were kicking a soccer ball around on the hotel's pitch and putt golf course.

The Lions had a week to recover from their long journey and prepare for their opening match of their twenty-five game tour on the following Wednesday. The New Zealanders, meanwhile, were beginning their preparations. Two trial matches were to be played at Wanganui to select the All Blacks team which they hoped would be good enough to start a new era in New Zealand rugby.

New Zealand rugby had never been so bad as in the 1970s. The most important task of the newly appointed coach Jack Gleeson was to find a captain to succeed No. 8 Andy Leslie, a replacement for line-out specialist and second row forward Peter Whiting, who had just retired, and a new full back.

Gleeson wanted to build a team that would last for some seasons and even experienced players such as Ian Kirkpatrick and Sid Going, with over sixty internationals between them, had no guarantee of selection.

The trials at Wanganui took the form of two games involving nearly seventy players. It was clear at the end that the All Blacks would have to come up with some astonishing new players if they were to discard Going, Kirkpatrick and one or two other senior men.

As the trials began a pall of black smoke went up over Wanganui. The Lions were not fooled. They knew it wasn't a funeral pyre for All Black rugby, despite all the moaning that New Zealanders had indulged in since the Lions arrived. It was instead the mark of a new era.

Chapter 5

Doc Murdoch and the liaison officers

When a Lion had some aches and pains, was bruised and cut, couldn't sleep or just felt stiff, he went to see Doc Murdoch, the masseur cum baggage man. He was a short and stocky New Zealander with weathered hands who lived amidst an unholy mess of boxes, crates, cartons, kitbags and trunks. Like matron's surgery, Doc's room was a veritable travelling hospital, a haven for the physically infirm and the mentally depressed.

In one corner of his room were three big white kitbags containing a soccer ball that Doc had first bought in 1971 and ten rugger balls. A long blue case, stamped with British Isles Rugby Union Tour, was open, and bandages, tape, scissors, jars and tubes spilled on to the floor. On a table near the window were little sachets of washers and studs, and on the floor by his bed stood two cardboard boxes of apples and oranges. In the middle of it all was Doc's portable massage table.

Murdoch was the hardest-working, most unobtrusive man on tour. He was usually the first down for breakfast and would begin his massage in the mid-afternoon before match days. The day after a game he wouldn't get any rest either. As the team moved on he first packed his medicaments and then all his other paraphernalia. Then he could start to supervise the transportation of the 110 pieces of Lions' luggage, weighing nearly 2½ tons. He did this unenviable task with infinite dedication at least fity times on tour.

The Lions would leave their baggage in the hotel foyer. Then an airline truck came to collect it all and Doc would not only help load it but would travel to the airport to see it put on the plane. At the other end he would supervise the unloading in the new hotel. Sometimes he even had to take all the baggage upstairs himself. It seemed a miracle that he, a man approaching 70, didn't have a heart attack on tour.

Doc made his first trip as baggage man cum masseur with the 1971 Lions. Since then he has done another thirteen tours, once four in one year, with teams from Romania, Fiji, Tonga, Western Samoa, Ireland, Scotland, and England. Of them all the most hectic was the All Blacks nine-match internal tour in 1972. 'We met on a Friday and played eight games in a fortnight – Saturday, Tuesday, Thursday, Saturday, Tuesday, Thursday and so on. We travelled by regular transport and sometimes had to wait up to three hours for a plane.'

Murdoch is an expert masseur but what makes him so good and popular is that, having been a top-class player, he understands the tensions and nerves players suffer. They come to him for massage beginning the afternoon before a match.

'I could start rubbing after tea and go until midnight,' says Doc, whose real christian name is Clive. 'I spend between three-quarters of an hour and one hour on each player, no trouble. Props get sore shoulders so I rub a little heat into them. The liniment I use is a proper muscular preparation, a methyl salicylate ointment. I generally rub it in the night before as it takes a while to work. The three quarters tend to want me to massage their hamstrings, calves and thighs.'

There is no end to his talents. Doc is the team's seamstress, sewing on buttons, darning torn jerseys, and if a player's boot is ripped then it is Doc who fixes it. He carries enough pills and medicines to stock a chemist's shop. He uses fourteen to sixteen rolls of white sticky elastoplast for each game. 'I use it as support for the ankles.' He carries crêpe bandages, knee bandages, chocolate flavoured nourishers and vitamin pills, as well as Mogadon sleeping pills and commonplace aspirins.

The morning of a match Doc Murdoch carefully laid out on the bed in his room the twenty-one sets of kit the players would need that afternoon. He put the shirts on the bottom, then the shorts, folded the stockings and neatly laid them on top. After their mid-morning team meeting the Lions came in to collect their kit. In the baggage he takes to every match are forty towels, ten cakes of soap, shampoo, a crate of milk and three or four dozen soft drinks. He has much more than he can carry but he declines help from the players. 'I get all my stuff ready and I like to handle it myself. Chaps come in and say, "I'll take this for you," and, "I'll take that for you," and you finish up not quite sure whether you've got everything.'

At each match Murdoch wore a red track suit and rugby boots; he sat on a bench near the touchline ready to run on to the field to attend to any injured player. In the changing room after the match he would hand out soap and towels and tend to any cuts and bruises.

Some New Zealanders found it hard to understand that Doc could work for a team playing against his countrymen. 'Someone from Auckland, my home, was saying to me just now how could I be a true Kiwi helping another team. It is an honour for me to be asked to do this job. When Jack Sullivan [former chairman of the council of the NZRFU] told me I had been specially asked for by the Lions I was very flattered. That has never happened before so I am honoured to be the first. If I am with the boys then I am with them 100 per cent. I feel for them. I worry for them. I understand them. I got pretty close to Elgan Rees when he hurt his leg. He's a young boy on his first tour and while he was injured I got to know him well. Then at last I saw him play his first game and that meant a lot to me.'

Murdoch has the sort of reassuring, understanding nature that makes other people want to take their problems to him and turn his room into the team's inner sanctum. George Burrell would always knock before entering Murdoch's room. Doc sat for hours talking to players and his home-made portable massage table often doubled as a psychiatrist's couch.

Murdoch became so popular with the Lions that they paid for him to fly to Fiji with them at the end of their tour. I have an abiding memory of Doc arriving at Nandi airport late on Sunday evening and wandering in among the crowds saying, '*Bula, Bula*' to everyone (*Bula* means hello). As soon as he got to the team hotel he sat in a chair, ordered a drink and shouted for John Dawes. There was just a hint of a twinkle in his eye when Dawes appeared. 'Where's my gear, John? You said I needn't lift a thing in Fiji.'

As the Lions moved around New Zealand they were accompanied by liaison officers provided by the NZRFU. There were three of them who took it in turns to look after the visiting team and were on duty for eight matches each: Russ Thomas, a silver-haired, fast-talking businessman from Christchurch, Peter Wild, whose brother was the Lord Chief Justice of New Zealand, and Pat Gill of Wellington.

A liaison officer's job covered a multitude of different tasks. He had to arrange transport for the team, make sure their accommodation was satisfactory, pay their weekly pocket money and lay on medical facilities. 'In short,' says Russ Thomas, 'a liaison officer's job is to sense what the players are all about.'

The liaison officer was the eyes and ears of the NZRFU and the most difficult of his tasks was to strike a delicate balance between the needs of the players and the budget allocated to him. He had to make sure the money the Lions spent was justified without seeming to the visitors to be stingy and parsimonious.

This was often very difficult but at times of disagreement there was a method of arbitration – the tours agreement signed by the seven International Board countries, the UK and Ireland, South Africa, Australia and New Zealand.

This agreement listed precisely what was payable and what was not. For example, morning coffee and afternoon tea were allowed but beer at meal times was not. A player's medical expenses were covered so long as he went to an NZRFU-approved doctor. Otherwise he had to make his own arrangements. By the letter of the law players were not allowed room service in their hotels nor wine with their meals.

There were many other outdated aspects to the tours agreement and I wondered why it had not been brought up to date. 'It is not desirable to have too much latitude in the agreement,' explained Thomas. 'It is much better to allow the liaison officers to use their own discretion.'

Although officially the only drink that had to be provided was in the team room, the Lions were served wine twice each week on match days. Normally one bottle was shared between four of them, sometimes one between two and on one memorable evening there were as many as 28 bottles.

At Hawke's Bay early in the tour the Lions had a good time. But Thomas blew his top when he discovered they were signing his name when ordering their drinks and he put a stop to it immediately. 'I never query laundry or dry-cleaning bills. The Lions can have all they want as well as morning coffee and afternoon tea. But drinks are only provided for the management.' The players found that very hard to understand. It seemed to them the NZRFU were being very mean towards them. The Lions were earning their hosts over £1 million (NZ$1.7 million). Why couldn't they have more free drinks?

The NZRFU were soft-hearted over other things. They allowed Allan Martin and Andy Irvine one free phone call home each week while their wives were pregnant.

The average weekly spending of a liaison officer was between NZ$4 000 (£2 350) and NZ$6 000 (£3 530). By far the larger part, between NZ$3 000 (£1 760) and NZ$4 000 (£2 350), went in paying the Lions' accommodation, food and laundry in their hotels. Then there was the week's pocket money of nearly NZ$2 000 (£1 176) that had to be paid to all the players and to the coach John Dawes but not manager George Burrell.

A liaison officer's day was filled with small but essential tasks. They had to allocate the players their allowance of tickets for provincial games: 55 free tickets and the right to buy another 20, for Test matches 65 free and the right to buy another 60. They had to arrange for transport to and from the physiotherapist, answer dozens of phone calls and arbitrate on the occasions of wrecking in hotels.

Early on in the tour a fire engine raced to the team hotel for a mysterious and unaccountable reason only to find no fire. Somebody had played the fool and it didn't need extensive investigations to find the culprit. The first time Russ Thomas took the joke in good humour and paid off the firemen. When it occurred again it wasn't so funny and the Lions had to find the money themselves. 'OK Mossy [Moss Keane], have your Guinness and I'll buy you a fire engine,' said manager George Burrell.

Chapter 6

Masterton: the first match

Masterton is a small farming town (population 5000) in the plain to the east of the Rimutaka and Tararu mountain ranges, 50 miles north-east of Wellington. The Lions were happy there. The Solway Park hotel where they stayed was a one-storey building set back from the main road with a heated swimming pool and a three-hole golf course at the back. The double rooms the Lions shared had black-and-white television sets and a pleasant view out over the golf course.

It was quiet and comfortable, the food was good and the weather, too. 'I've been telling the boys about the crummy hotels and lousy weather in New Zealand,' said Derek Quinnell, remembering his visit with the Lions in 1971. At the time a warm autumn sun was glinting on the water in the pool, the mountains Quinnell had never seen because of thick mist and rain when he was last in Masterton, stood out firm and clear, and only a light breeze blew down from the hills.

At the Solway Park, as in all the hotels they stayed in, the Lions had a special room stacked with beer and soft drinks. This was where the team gathered when they wanted to be alone, where they held their team talks before their opening game and their celebratory sing-song after it. This was their room and no one else was allowed in without permission. There were also boxes of apples and other fruit that farmers brought in from the rich lands all around.

Training was the central event of the day. Players would gather soon after breakfast and then go by coach to a local school. The venues for training were always varied from day to day so the prestige of having the Lions train on their ground was allowed to as many clubs and schools as possible.

'Training is a matter of using the ball and making it competitive,' explained John Dawes after lunch one afternoon. 'The game is easy. My problem is to make training more interesting.'

The first day all the Lions did was to play soccer, touch rugby and Gaelic football. Soon, though, training became more serious. Phil Bennett took the backs, which left Dawes able to concentrate on the forwards. Dawes spent a lot of time asking questions and encouraging players to give their answers. 'Nine times out of ten I know the answer myself but I want to know what the players think themselves.' He was assessing which of them were capable of taking future scrummaging sessions and of becoming a pack leader.

The injuries that were to affect the party so much began even before they left Britain. Bobby Windsor trod in a pothole while running with club-mate Terry Cobner near their homes in Newport and his right leg was so stiff he couldn't train at Masterton. He went to have special treatment one day. 'The chap poked and prodded and pulled at my leg for ten minutes,' said Windsor the same evening. 'Then he told me, "You've got a bad leg". He was hopeless, that one.' And Windsor shook his head despairingly. 'Bloody hopeless. I'm going to train tomorrow anyway. Sod it.'

A definite training pattern began to emerge. Most sessions would begin with running around the pitch to warm up, usually groups of five interpassing the ball as they ran. Dawes called his men around him. 'The man with the ball has to sprint when I blow the whistle,' he said. 'One blast means sprint forward, two blasts means run ten yards backwards. Three blasts means jump in the air. Off you go.' One! Three! Two! Dawes paced around the field as he supervised this exercise.

'Right,' he said. 'Same groups of five as before. I want you all to run down to the other end of the field, touch the goal-line, turn around and run back to me. The last group must do it again.'

The big forwards Fran Cotton, Allan Martin, Clive Williams, Bobby Windsor and Gordon Brown all had to do it again, while the others stood watching, their hands on their hips, grateful for the rest.

Next Dawes ordered his men to pair off and do wheelbarrows. 'Pusher try and push the barrow over the goal line,' Dawes

shouted. 'Barrow, try to stop him.' The players were beginning
to sweat in the sun.

'Come on Panther and Broonie,' Dawes shouted at Martin
and Brown. The two second row forwards were lumbering their
way towards the goal-line in a wheelbarrow, Martin the wheels
and Brown the pusher.

Soon they would split into forwards and backs. Dawes led the
forwards over to the scrummaging machine, a medieval device
through which the prop forwards and hooker put their heads
and shoulders. The other five forwards packed down normally
behind them. On the other side of the scrum was a platform on
which the other forwards stood to weigh the machine down.

'Come on, Panther. I'll put my foot up your backside. People
are working here,' Dawes shouted at Martin.

The scrum broke up. Derek Quinnell shook his head. 'No
snap,' he said, looking worried and wiping the sweat from his
face. 'Moss, you and Panther are much too loose as you go down.
Get together.'

They went down for the tenth time. 'If it's good this will be
the last one,' said Dawes, adding quickly, '*if* it's good.'

The backs meanwhile had been having a penalty-kicking
competition. Now the backs and forwards came together again.
Dawes ordered everyone behind the goal-line and he walked to
stand on the 25 facing them. He ordered the players to sprint to
him and then jog back.

'Let's walk back, Syd,' said Bennett.

'Jog,' said Dawes firmly. He moved to the halfway line and
the players sprinted to him. Brynmor Williams, the scrum half,
and the wing J.J. Williams were the first to reach him. Dawes
moved back to the 25 and over the shorter distance Bennett and
J.J. Williams were the fastest. Dawes retired further from the
players until, finally, after six more sprints he was right up at the
other end of the pitch, legs apart, whistle in his mouth. He gave
one short peep and then closely watched the players racing
towards him.

Elgan Rees on the left was moving quickly but so was J.J.
Williams on the right. In the centre Andy Irvine and Mike
Gibson were together. Right at the back were Quinnell, Windsor and Moss Keane. As the players reached him Dawes shouted
out, 'Well done!' and gave them two minutes rest. Then Fran

Cotton, a physical education teacher, took over. 'I want you to do three sets of press-ups, burpees and abdominals, ten in each set,' he ordered. 'Nobody is checking on you other than yourself. If you can't do ten press-ups then you bloody well shouldn't be here. Keep your legs straight,' he shouted as out of the corner of his eye he saw someone doing abdominals with very bent knees.

As the men sweated in the sun Dawes walked quietly among them, his hands behind his back, a smile playing around his face. 'Finished?' he asked Bobby Windsor and Clive Williams who had been doing the stomach exercises side by side. 'Off you go then,' and the two forwards trudged wearily to the shower. Sessions like that often took over two hours.

Back in the hotel the Lions gratefully swigged up to forty pints of milk and guzzled deliciously crisp apples while they autographed the books, balls, and team photographs that were always lying around for them at the hotel reception desk. After lunch they would split into groups and go golfing, shooting, or doing any of the half dozen activities that were laid on for them.

Allan Martin went duck shooting and bagged a black swan, as well as nearly shooting off his own foot. Doug Morgan dazzled two ladies with whom he was playing golf by covering twelve holes in three over fours.

Burrell and Dawes both claimed they were swimming in the heated pool at 6.30 one morning. At other times Dawes battled over the hotel's pitch and putt course with Derek Quinnell, another in their continuing series of competitions that had begun with crib on the plane. So far it was one victory each at squash and Quinnell was leading his coach at cards. But the big man's golf was letting him down. 'I played well today though,' he said, the night before the first game. 'Syd only beat me three and one.'

Alex McDonald arrived to join the Lions at Masterton. McDonald, a slight, distinguished-looking man with a diffident manner and soft voice, was going to be the tour secretary. He had fulfilled this role since 1966 when he retired from government service. His main job was to help George Burrell with his correspondence, for which he was paid a nett of NZ$65 a week by the NZRFU. He would accept or decline invitations on behalf of the Lions and then send out the thank you cards engraved with the Four Home Unions' crest. He was also responsible for having all the plaques, ties, pins, badges ready for George Burrell to hand out at after-match functions. 'This is my third Lions tour,' explained McDonald. 'For me it is an honour and privilege. I like the four-day stops because they give me time to work. I can get a lot done on Monday, Tuesday and Wednesday. Thursday is given up to travelling and Friday I do a couple of hours' work. Saturday is the game, and then Sunday we move on again.'

The first thing he did when he arrived at Masterton was to go to a local printer with a sheet of specimens of all the Lions signatures and had 10 000 copies made. That cost the four home unions N Z $176. They were to be sent out to schoolchildren and fans who wrote to the Lions. 'In 1966 the Lions brought out several thousand sheets of autographs but they were incomplete. In 1971 they did a lot on the plane but there were one or two signatures missing even from those. I used to have to spend a lot of time collecting autographs from the Lions for people who wrote in but that was no good. At the end of the tour all the boys remembered was that I was the intrusive person who kept pestering them for autographs. The job has more dignity than that.'

He was a busy man who used to walk around carrying his typewriter in a brown case stamped with N Z R F U. At each hotel he would type out copies of the accommodation pairings and then circulate them around the team. He was a friendly man too, and often helped the players with their fan mail.

He looked an incongruous sight in his pork pie hat, blazer and flannels and shining shoes, overcoat folded neatly over his arm, carrying a battered old brown cardboard box piled high with letters and envelopes all held together with bits of string.

While McDonald was busy at the printers, Burrell, Dawes and Bennett held their first selection meeting. The team they chose for the opening game against Wairarapa-Bush was: Hay; Squires, McGeechan, Burcher, J.J. Williams; Bennett (Capt.), B. Williams; No. 8 Quinnell; T. Evans, Horton, Keane, T. Cobner; Price, Wheeler, Orr. Of the forwards all but Quinnell were new Lions, and Hay, Squires, Burcher and Brynmor Williams were new Lions in the backs.

Wairarapa-Bush, captained by George Nepia's grandson Bill

Graham Price bloodied, battered but never bowed. He did Pontypool, Wales and Britain proud.

Jack Gleeson points it out but John Dawes seems to be disagreeing. They disagreed rather a lot. They called a truce in the end.

Top left: *Balletically Bennett looks perfect. Another glorious touch-finder.* Above: *Training was always hard and not often in the sunshine.*

Below: *Before the first Test, Tane Norton looked stern. Later he was a delighted, victorious captain.*

'Please Syd can I stop now,' prays Brynmor Williams to coach John (Syd) Dawes in training.

Not only the players became muddied oafs. Referee Harrison picked up his fair share of mud at Westport.

Stomach exercises are easier when team-mates can help, though Peter Wheeler, nearest camera, looks exhausted all the same.

Rowlands, scored two tries in their spirited, wind-assisted first half. The weather had changed overnight and it was bitterly cold, and sleet was driving down the pitch into the Lions' faces in the first half. Yet when the local side led by only 13–12 at half time it was clear they had nothing to match the power of the Lions forwards or the speed and handling of the Lions backs. Wing J.J. Williams scored three tries and the other wing, Peter Squires, got one. In all the Lions three quarters scored six of the team's eight tries. The Lions' pleasure at their 41–13 victory was marred only by the concussion Nigel Horton suffered after being punched by Ian Turley at a line out early on. The big Birmingham policeman fell to the ground like a boxer and was led from the field with blood pouring from his left eye. He spent the night in hospital with concussion.

They sang well in the team room that night. The choirmaster was Gordon Brown. 'I am probably the worst singer in the party but I was asked to be choirmaster because I know roughly when guys feel like singing and when they don't. The first sing-song we had at Richmond the boys were all dead reluctant to sing. This is definitely the most reluctant singing team I have ever been with.' The Lions improved their singing considerably during the tour and just before the third Test EMI made a record of them. It hasn't yet reached the hit parade.

The purpose of singing on tour is to unite the party and help them relax after a game. As soon as they got back to their hotel after a match the players and the management would go straight into the team room, shut the door, and not reappear until they had finished their sing-song, sometimes as much as two hours later. The songs were washed down by cans and cans of beer. 'We never feel any closer on tour than in the team room after a match,' says Brown.

The singing was an important part of the tour and had to be properly organized. 'As soon as we got together in Richmond I told the boys that they each should choose their own song. I told them to think about it on the plane so I could make a list of the songs when we were in Masterton.

'There was only one night when we actually sang at Richmond and there was a tremendous feeling for *Flower of Scotland* to be the team song. The Scottish boys sing it because it has got a bit of feeling to it, and the Welsh boys sing it on their way to their games. I had to steer them away from choosing it as the team song because it was the official team song and we have to have an identity of our own. What is past is past.' So they chose *Country Road* by John Denver, which everybody liked.

> Almost heaven, West Virginia,
> Blue Ridge Mountain, Shenandoah River,
> Life is older, older than the trees,
> Younger than the mountains,
> Growing like the breeze.
>
> Country Road, take me home
> To the place where I belong;
> West Virginia, mountain mama,
> Take me home Country Road.

Other favourites included *Flower of Scotland, Island of Dreams, Jet Plane, Last Thing on My Mind* and *The Leaving of Liverpool.*

Sometimes they didn't feel like singing immediately if their spirits were low. So they played games like buzz and bunnies, tests of mental dexterity. Anybody who made a mistake had to drink a glass of beer, and if anyone had to leave the room then he was forced to drink a glass of beer as a punishment before being allowed back in again. 'Within a half hour of playing everyone is stoned,' says Brown. 'It's great fun and games and as soon as anyone makes a mistake we all point the finger and roar at him. You always have a chairman no matter what game you are playing, and he has the final decision on who made what mistake and who has to drink a forfeit. The chairman is allowed to pick on people and say he must drink such and such. When you speak to the chair you must put your hand on your head. If you don't, you have to drink another glass of beer.'

Like soldiers returning from a battlefield the Lions needed these sessions to raise their spirits after slogging through the mud, wind and icy rain that dogged them throughout New Zealand.

Chapter 7

Colin Meads: coach of the future?

The one-storey wooden house was painted yellow and on the verandah at the front were three easy chairs beneath a line full of washing. Around the back eight dogs barked in their kennels and as they jumped against the wire mesh that confined them the noise echoed across the still afternoon.

In the shed down by the roadside a boy who looked to be 16 or 17 stood working with a part of an engine. He had slashes of oil on his suntanned face and greasy fingers from where he had pulled the troublesome part from under the bonnet.

The house belonged to Colin Meads, the legendary All Black, and the boy tending the truck was his oldest son Kelvin. It was the same house that Meads's father once lived in. A few years ago people used to drive miles just to see where their hero lived. Then, without getting out of their cars, they would turn around and drive home again.

At 41, Colin Meads is no longer the world's best-known rugby player as he was in the 1950s and 1960s when he played fifty-five Test matches for his country. Instead he is making a name for himself as a rugby coach, while continuing to run his 2000 acres of mainly sheep farm, and fulfilling the demands made on him as President of the King Country branch of the society of mentally handicapped children.

Down in Taumarunui, a country town of 5000 people fifty miles to the south, Meads was leading the King Country/Wanganui team in their first training run. They were to meet the Lions in two days. It was raining heavily and the rivers Wanganui and Ongarui, which raced along each side of the ground, were swollen almost to their banks. Perhaps training should be abandoned, a visitor suggested diffidently. 'Why?' asked Meads, surprised at the very thought. 'It could be raining during the game, too.'

For training Meads wore black shorts, his All Black stockings and an All Black track suit top over a white shirt. He jogged slowly around the pitch, his head down, shouting out instructions in a gruff voice. For two hours he gave them line-out practice, rucking and driving. He swore a lot, constantly needling one player and then another. He made them practise rucking the ball back and then he ordered the stand off to kick it high back into the box in front of the forwards so the forwards could run onto it and ruck it back. Then the whole exercise could start again. They ended the session lining up at one end of the field and passing the ball as fast as possible while running to the other end of the pitch. The rain still pelted down.

Meads is a very successful newcomer to coaching. He started with King Country in 1976 and lifted them from bottom to third in the ten-team second division of the provincial championship in one year. The game against the Lions was to be his biggest test so far. 'Our problem here is that we have so few players to choose from,' Meads explained after that first training run. 'Our whole area doesn't have as many people as Hamilton and so we find it very hard to find big men.'

The next morning Meads held another training session, this time a short one and he concentrated on scrummaging. 'If the Lions drive, you go across the field,' he shouted at his second row forwards. 'That stops them going forward.' The scrum broke up. 'You see what happens is that you end up being pushed across the field and there is nothing too bad about that.'

He ordered them down for another scrum. It collapsed as the forwards tried to gain a grip on the soaking turf. 'You all right, Ray?' Meads asked his captain, Ray Stafford. 'You've got to keep talking to these buggers otherwise they will fall asleep.'

Meads moved on to another ploy. 'Let's practise getting the ball in quick,' he said. The scrum half Sammy Pye, a small weatherbeaten man, put the ball in quickly two or three times. Meads stood silently behind his scrum-half. Then he shouted, 'That's enough fellas. That's good. Curly will shout you' [buy a drink].

Curly Neilsen is a small balding man who always wears a hat.

He discovered Colin Meads and was sole selector and coach in the days when Meads captained King Country. The two of them became close friends and Neilsen is now honourary manager of the combined team.

'Colin played his first games as flanker or lock,' Neilson recalled later over a glass of beer. 'He was rough, raw-boned. Soon he became captain and from about 1960 or 1961 he took over the coaching of the forwards as well. He was a great leader, specially of the younger players. He was their hero and they were dedicated to him. They worshipped him.'

Everybody seemed to worship Meads and an enormous shock went around the communities of Te Kuite, where Meads lives, and Taumarunui when they heard that Meads had broken his back in a car accident. 'The bottom just dropped out of my world . . . out of my universe,' recalls Neilsen.

The local journalist Eric Clarke remembers it well. 'I have a King Country page in the *Daily News* but this was a front-page story. It was a national calamity. You would walk down the street and all you would hear would be people saying to one another, "Did you hear what happened to Piney. Do you think it is the end of his career?"'

The accident happened late one Saturday evening in December 1971. It had been a very hot day and Meads and some rugby friends had spent most of it painting the roof of a supermarket in Te Kuite to raise money for their rugby club, Waitete.

About eleven Meads climbed into his Land Rover, exhausted and sunburnt, to drive the few miles to his home. He got to within one hundred yards of the road leading down to his house when he fell asleep at the wheel. His Land Rover ploughed straight on into some scrub. Two bottles of champagne that he had bought for his daughter Shelley's christening the next day went out of one window; he went out of the other. The steering wheel was forced into the back of the driver's seat.

His wife Verna Meads was getting ready for bed when she heard the news. 'A chap came up the road laughing and grinning – with nerves I later realized. I couldn't understand what he was trying to tell me about Colin. Colin had always seemed so indestructible. But then he showed me Colin's watch. It was shattered. That convinced me.'

When Meads came to in hospital the next morning his first

thought was to get up to milk the cows. Semi-conscious, he struggled out of bed and collapsed on the floor, the drips attached to his arm flying all over the ward. Then came the shock. 'I couldn't move at all,' he recalls. 'I was totally helpless, dependent on others.'

Meads was out of hospital by Christmas, plastered from the neck down to the groin, able only to lie down or stand up. While supposedly convalescing he broke this plaster cast around him no less than three times, once shearing a sheep. The day it finally came off he began training for rugby by going for a run and two months later he was playing again.

As with many people who brush with death, Meads became aware of his frailties after his accident. He had always been a humble, quiet and shy man; now he became more aware of people who were mentally or physically less able than he was. 'That accident made me think how lucky I was. I could have been paralysed for ever.'

A couple of years later when he was asked to become President of the King Country branch of the charity looking after mentally handicapped children he accepted with pleasure. He talks proudly now of helping to raise N Z $22 000 to build a workshop for the mentally handicapped in Otorohanga. When he is asked to attend functions, to speak at dinners, he generally asks that a fee be paid to the mentally handicapped.

When I met Colin Meads I was struck by his sheer physical size, the size of his hands and the brusqueness of his welcome. Yet I sensed that the brusqueness was not a lack of warmth but an inability to make himself at ease with a complete stranger. 'He is still rather a shy man who believes he owes a lot to football,' says Verna.

As an All Black Colin Mead has visited countries he had only read about, met people he would otherwise never meet. He is a Member of the British Empire. He has met the Queen of England several times, been to the Houses of Parliament, drunk champagne in the Casino de Paris. Were it not for his rugby he would have been just another farmer in a nation of sheep farmers.

Since he launched himself in the latest phase of his career he has had to acquire some of the finesse he did not need in earlier days. He still tends to talk in well-worn phrases but he has learned to talk more fully and easily. He rarely turns down journalists who want an interview.

Many rugby followers in Britain and Australia remember Colin Meads for his violence. He knocked out Welshman David Watkins. He hit Jeff Young, breaking Young's jaw, because the Welsh hooker had committed the rugby crime of pulling a jersey. Kenny Catchpole's misfortune was to be caught in a ruck head down, one leg protruding like a ship's mast from amidst the heaving bodies. Meads grabbed it, ripped it as he might a chicken bone and the Australian's international career had virtually ended.

'I don't think anyone plays for a country as long as I did and remains popular everywhere,' says Meads now when faced with a reminder of his misdeeds. 'You don't play it to make yourself popular, do you?'

'But do you have any remorse?' I asked him.

'For some of them you do. The David Watkins episode for example. We've spoken about it since so I am not breaking any confidences if I tell you that he toppled over after I hit him. I reckon he was only acting. I'm saying to myself, "Come on you little bastard" and then everyone starts booing you.'

'And Catchpole?'

'In Australia my name stinks because Catchy was their idol. He had the ball, he was caught in a ruck and we were trying to get the ball off him so I grabbed one leg to tip him over onto the ground. How was I to know his other leg was stuck? It wasn't my fault the other leg was trapped between two bodies and he virtually did the splits and tore his groin muscles very badly. Catchy and I have spoken to one another since. We toured in Tonga together. There is no malice between us.'

There is no malice between referee Kevin Kelleher and Meads either. At Murrayfield in 1967 when Scotland faced the touring All Blacks, Kelleher sent off the New Zealander for dangerous play. The following Christmas Kelleher sent Meads a Christmas card and one arrives at Te Kuite each Christmas even now.

For a time after being sent off Meads felt nothing but shame, as did Verna, sitting up in bed 12 000 miles away listening to a crackly radio commentary. For the next few days she seemed unable to turn on the television without seeing a reconstruction of the incident. 'If I saw it once on television I saw it fifty million times. It nearly drove me demented.' She was soothed by an outburst of support for her husband from the Prime Minister of New Zealand, from people in Te Kuite and all over the country. One even came from Wales. It was signed, 'From two and a half million Welshmen, bad luck.'

Mead's playing career is over now but his fame survives. Journalists want to interview him and children write from all over the world wanting his autograph. There is a street in Te Kuite named after him, a racehorse called Pine Tree and a house called Meads House in a local reform school.

He knows but does not understand the price of fame and wonders whether his children have even begun to learn to live with it. He worries most about Kelvin, his eldest son, more than Karen, who is the oldest, and Rhonda, Glynn and Shelley. 'It is hard for them to be Colin Meads's children. My sons have to do their own thing. I keep well away from their rugby but they've got to learn to adapt. Kelvin finds it hard even when he is injured. People say to him, "What the hell is wrong with you. Your father was never injured." '

It was now 12.15 on the morning of the match against the Lions. We had been talking much too long and Meads had to get back to his team. I asked him a last question: what would happen that afternoon?

'We'll be terribly proud if we hold the Lions to 30 points. I'd like to see the brilliance of Phil Bennett because I know that little bugger and how brilliant he can be. But I won't let my team think that. I'll be telling them for God's sake don't let him get away.'

Gamely as his men tried, they couldn't stop the Lions running in eleven tries, Bennett scoring his first of the tour and converting all but three. It was the Lions' biggest victory on tour. Despite the big defeat, Meads was pleased with his team. They had run the ball as he had taught them to and as Fred Allen had taught him to a decade earlier, and they scored the last try with a brilliant inter-passing movement that went from one end of the pitch to the other. 'For these fellows this was the game of a lifetime,' said Meads after the match. 'I wanted them to enjoy it and they did.'

Ray Stafford, the tall, lean flanker, had run his heart out all afternoon and he relished his beer in the Memorial Hall after the game. 'The thing about Piney,' said the team captain, 'is that he seems able to hand down years of experience to you in moments. He said the Lions would come from anywhere and kill the ball. He said this would happen, that would happen during the game and when it did you thought to yourself, "Oh, shit, that's just like old PT said it would." '

Chapter 8

The first defeat

Pressure, pressure, pressure was the plan of New Zealand Universities captain Doug Rollerson as his men ran onto the pitch at Lancaster Park Oval, Christchurch, for their game against the British Lions. It was the Tuesday before the first Test between the Lions and the All Blacks, and the outcome of the Universities game would inevitably be taken as an indication of what might happen at Wellington on Saturday.

The students had had two warm-up games and had spent one week together in preparation for this match. The Lions had a lot of injury problems, and there had been odd aspects to the play right from the start. Following their brilliant performance in the opening match there was the other, less acceptable side to their game against Hawke's Bay, three days later. The weather in Napier was good, the ground firm and the Lions sped into a lead of 13–0. So far so good but then they nearly threw it away by allowing the Bay to score two good tries within five minutes and to close to within 2 points.

At Manawatu the Lions were trailing 9–0 after twenty minutes before staging a desperate revival and nosing ahead with twenty minutes remaining. There had been a narrow squeak against Otago the previous Wednesday when, outscored by one try to none, outrucked and outwitted, the Lions had won only because Phil Bennett kicked four penalty goals. Then down at Invercargill it was an hour before the Lions could shake off a dogged but limited Southland side.

Except in easy matches the Lions were very slow starters. The trouble seemed to be in the forwards. They had not yet found a pack leader, and they were still weak and disorganized in their line-out work. Even the scrummaging was not wholly satisfactory. By selecting five walking wounded players for the team against the Universities the Lions were taking a calculated risk.

Full back Bruce Hay injured his ankle against Southland. Flanker Tony Neary also had an injured ankle and Derek Quinnell was still bothered by a bad leg. Wing Elgan Rees was playing only his third game of the tour after tearing a hamstring in training before the first match. And scrum half Doug Morgan had not played for a fortnight since he had badly injured his ribs against King Country/Wanganui two weeks earlier.

From the kick off the students followed their captain's plan perfectly. Flankers Ray Scott and Denis Thorn pressurized scrum half Morgan so much that he could rarely get his pass to his stand off John Bevan as quickly as he would have liked. This in turn slowed down the Lions three quarters. The students were also able to stand up to the Lions forwards who had not yet developed the correct tactics nor discovered the awesome power in their scrummaging that was to come later. In fact the Lions forwards were sloppy.

Universities full back Doug Heffernan and captain Rollerson were both kicking outstandingly well. They inspired their team-mates by kicking three penalties between them to give their side a lead of 9-3 at half time.

Immediately after half time though the Lions scored a try. The ball popped out of the side of the Universities scrum and Neary scooped it up, passed to Quinnell who burst over the line with two men on his back to score the first try of the game. The Lions now held the initiative but lost it immediately when Rollerson kicked a penalty after Moss Keane had punched an opponent.

A massive penalty attempt from 52 yards by Doug Morgan may have gone over the bar. The Universities players thought it did and so did some of the Lions. One touch judge agreed and held his flag up but the other kept his down and the referee adjudged the penalty kick missed.

Perhaps the Lions had a justifiable grievance but a few minutes later Universities stand off Paul McFie scored a try nearly under the posts after several forward charges and a quick heel from a scrum. That was the end. The Lions were out of it, outplayed and out-thought.

Gordon Brown went off with an injured shoulder, hurt when a Universities player landed on it, and Allan Martin came on instead. Later Moss Keane went off with concussion. By this time the Lions had no more second row forwards and the best way of replacing Keane was for Phil Orr to come on and go to loose head prop, which he did, while Fran Cotton moved back into the second row.

Nothing could save the Lions now, not even a rash of penalties against the Universities. The entire Universities team had played above themselves, notably Rollerson and Heffernan and scrum half Mark Romans, who looked to the Lions to be as much of a threat as Terry Burcher had down at Otago. For once a New Zealand team outkicked the Lions. Heffernan and Rollerson shared the goal kicking and between them landed five penalties and one conversion out of ten kicks at goal. Two of the failures rebounded off the posts.

So ended a run of thirty-nine successive matches without defeat for the Lions, stretching back to the second Test on the same ground in 1971. 'We are not having a party,' said John Dawes sourly when asked what the team would be doing that evening. Phil Bennett did not lose his sense of diplomacy completely. 'It could prove a timely lesson for the team and help us in our preparations for the Test in the next few days,' said the captain. 'At least we will no longer be the favourites.'

Chapter 9

First Test –
Lions 12 All Blacks 16

A stern-faced George Burrell announced the team for the first Test the morning after the New Zealand Universities game. It was: Irvine, Squires, McGeechan, Fenwick, J.J. Williams, P. Bennett (Capt.), Brynmor Williams, Duggan, Trevor Evans, Cobner (pack leader), Keane, Martin, Price, Windsor, Orr. Replacements were Hay, Gareth Evans, Morgan, Cotton, Wheeler and Quinnell.

It was a team dominated by Welshmen – five forwards and four backs. Even for the first two Tests in New Zealand six years earlier there had been only eight Welshmen.

The rise of Wales marked the end of the links with 1971, for not a player remained from that time. Mike Gibson couldn't even get into the replacements, which was a surprise. Four backs remained from the victorious team in South Africa in 1974, but only one forward – Bobby Windsor the hooker from Pontypool – and there were questions as to whether he was a better all-round player than the Englishman Peter Wheeler.

Injuries dictated many of the selections among the forwards. The big Scot Gordon Brown would have been a certainty as the main line-out jumper but he had injured his right shoulder against the Universities when a player following up a kick off landed on his shoulder with both feet. Most probably Nigel Horton would have been his partner in the second row had he not broken his thumb. Horton's replacement, Billy Beaumont from Fylde in Lancashire, had not recovered from his thirty-hour flight from London, and the selectors had to call on the only two available locks left – Moss Keane for the front of the line and Allan Martin. It was a Celtic partnership.

There were some doubts about Keane's availability. Under

ideal circumstances he should have been rested for a week after being concussed against the Universities. But these were desperate times, not ideal circumstances. He had to play. There was no one else available.

Or was there? Perhaps Derek Quinnell could have played instead. Certainly the Welsh forward who had played well on tour should have been picked somewhere in the forwards. Trevor Evans was faster around the field than the big Llanelli player but he had none of Quinnell's expertise in the whirlpool of arms and elbows that is the line out. Quinnell would have been excellent at No. 6 in the line out, as he proved in the second and third Tests. By omitting him the selectors left Willie Duggan at the back of the line completely unprotected, which meant Duggan was going to have great difficulty in winning any ball at all.

Yet from the Lions' point of view the most important player was Brynmor Williams, the scrum half. Williams had been selected for the Lions to universal acclaim but once in New Zealand his lack of international experience showed. He could be a matchwinner but he could make the most horrible mistakes. Had Doug Morgan, the other scrum half, not been injured he might have posed a greater threat to his rival. Doug's virtues of experience and steadiness were just what Brynmor lacked.

A clearance kick of Williams's was charged down at Wairarapa-Bush in the opening game of the tour and led to the first try against the Lions. At Invercargill against Southland he had a day that was typical of his play up to then. He mixed it with the Southland forwards, gymnastically throwing himself hither and yon, and gutsily soaking up punishment in rucks and mauls. At the same time though, his passing to his captain was occasionally awry and often slow. He could throw the ball a long way, could kick well and he was faster in the break than his mentor at Cardiff, Gareth Edwards. But with his relatively big backswing he was often caught out in the mud of New Zealand. Worst of all, he had a tendency to make one bad error in each game.

The trouble was he was so nervous and shy, manifestly in the shadow of Edwards, and the more he was compared with Edwards the more nervous he became. At times early in the tour he looked a rather lonely figure, as though he was haunted by a spectre.

'A lot of attention has been focussed on Doug and me,' he said one afternoon, 'and comparisons have been made with Gareth. I don't think they are fair. You have got to judge players on what they are. People say I should run a bit more. You can't put the ball into a scrum and say I am going to run now. A break just comes.

'It isn't that I've got an extra second, so I think shall I kick or shall I run or shall I pass? It's not that. My main fault is that I have got to learn to temper my over-eagerness. Over here I seem so conscious of doing well and wanting to do well. I have felt that so far in some of my games I have had patches when I have not done anything wrong, patches of twenty or twenty-five minutes. Then all of a sudden I fumble a ball behind a scrum. I think that it is inexperience. I am trying to make a break before I pick the ball up – that sort of thing.

'I was quite happy after the first game I played. At other times I have had a few shaky moments in some of the games but there is no point in me brooding too much over it, because if I start brooding it is going to affect me even more. I've just got to forget it and get on with it.

'I wouldn't say that it was hard for me to stop brooding. It depends on how you are as a person. If you are emotional, if you care, then you worry. I admit I am a bit of a worrier. I am emotional. I come from a very small village in West Wales – I'm proud of it, mind – and people from there do tend to be sensitive, to worry more than most. It's back to experience. That is a great leveller.'

At 25 Williams was too old to be comforted and treated as a raw youngster yet too inexperienced to be able to understand what was happening to him. He had to work it out for himself. The encouraging thing for the Lions was that he was showing signs of doing just that. He did seem to be steadying up.

It was cold and wet in Wellington when the Lions flew in from Christchurch and they went straight to the St George, a big, old-fashioned hotel on Willis Street. They trained at Athletic Park for two hours on the windy Thursday morning and then John Dawes called it a day. The All Blacks meanwhile slunk out of their hotel early to confuse journalists. Asked by a journalist if he knew the whereabouts of the All Blacks, the superintendent of the Wellington City transport department replied laconically, 'No. I hope you find them by Saturday.'

They were eventually tracked down on the fields of a school north of Wellington near a hotel that was owned by Jack Gleeson and his business associates. The All Blacks team had been announced by Ces Blazey, the chairman of the New Zealand Rugby Union, after the game between Otago and the Lions at Carisbrook, Dunedin, the previous week.

The team for the first Test of the first major series to be played in New Zealand for six years was national news. TV lights blazed down on the silver-haired former insurance broker, neat in a grey suit, as he read out the names that selectors Eric Watson and John Stewart and coach Gleeson had just finished selecting in an unlit unheated caravan. Radio microphones were poised to transmit the team.

One name stunned those present – Colin Farrell, an untried 21-year-old from Auckland whose rags to riches rise was so quick that one month earlier he hadn't been considered good enough to play in the All Black trials. He was described as a running full back. The only other new cap was Lawrie Knight, the doctor from Poverty Bay whom the All Blacks nicknamed Spock during their tour of South Africa in 1976. The selectors had resisted the clamour to replace flanker Ian Kirkpatrick and scrum half Sid Going with younger men.

The man with the least enviable task was Bryan Williams. On a ground that could pass as a wind tunnel most days, the swarthy Samoan was entrusted with all the goal kicking and not just the long ones, the hit and hopers, as he had been in South Africa. It was strange that only in his eighth year as an All Black should Williams be considered the best kicker in the team. Yet it did show how desperate the All Blacks were for kickers.

Wellington is sometimes called the windy city. Its steep hills with houses perched one on top of another, its gashing inlets and jutting headlands combine to attract every breath of wind from Cook Strait. Sometimes in the Windy City they have to string ropes on the pavements so pedestrians won't be blown into the road.

It rained and rained. On Thursday I awoke to the drumming of rain on my window. On Friday it was the same and on Saturday, too.

> Earth has not anything to show less fair:
> Dull would be he of soul who could pass by
> A sight so tattered in its majesty.

Denis Glover's words from a poem called *Wellington on a wet Sunday* applied just as much to the city on a wet Thursday, Friday and Saturday.

The rain wiped out the golf that Gordon Brown and Billy Beaumont had arranged for Friday morning with the Governor General because the course was waterlogged. The rain might have saved the Governor General some money, for though Brown has an official handicap of 17 at Troon he plays to about 11. 'I am a bandit off 17,' he admits.

The Test team had lunch secretly in a men's club and afterwards relaxed for three hours playing pool. Back in their hotel rooms they watched television while outside in the rain the traffic slowed to a crawl. Wellington was beginning to fill up with visitors from out of town coming in for the Test. The extra traffic on rain-slicked streets caused thirty-five accidents between mid-afternoon on Friday and one o'clock Saturday morning.

I spent Friday evening at Marist St Pats rugby club in Haitaitai Park, the former club of Joe Karam and Grant Batty, two All Blacks, and Ivan Vodanovich, who had coached the 1971 All Blacks. It was my first experience of the intensity with which New Zealanders take their rugby. Seventy men had paid NZ$11 (£6.50) to come and eat cold chicken, turkey and fruit salad and then listen to a Pom gibe them the inside poop about rugby. It hardly seemed worth it.

They put me in front of a lectern with a microphone, as if I was reading the lesson in Wellington Cathedral. I talked for ten minutes, then they fired questions at me. 'Why do the Lions' backs stand off side?' was the opener. Not bad I thought to myself. No false courtesies here. 'Weren't the All Blacks cheated in South Africa?' was the next. For twenty-five minutes I faced a firing squad. At the end of it, as I was driven back to my hotel through rain that was coming down more heavily than ever, I reckoned I knew and understood the New Zealand man better.

He was critical, outspoken, honest, and if you met his standards, he was warm-hearted. They made me sing for my supper and having done so I was presented with a handsome book about New Zealand and a club tie. Then they made me feel emotional as they burst into *For He's a Jolly Good Fellow* just before I left. For some time after that I felt that rugby was a good game to be part of.

The rain did stop and at 2.25 on Saturday afternoon Phil Bennett led his Lions out onto a wet and soggy Athletic Park, chucking Leo the mascot to Tony Neary, who was duty boy and was wrapped up inside his wet suit.

The wind was blowing straight up from the Arctic, that is from left to right to those in the main stand; Bennett, having won the toss, elected to play with it in the first half. The Lions made a wonderful start. At the first line out, five yards inside the All Blacks own half, an All Black stepped offside. Andy Irvine landed the goal. Play had been going for less than one minute.

But then came the first of the Lions' mistakes. As early as the fifth minute they allowed Sid Going in for a soft try. After a ruck ten yards from the Lions line, the scrum half looked to his right and then to his left. His hesitancy, untypical as it was, fooled some of the Lions and some went left and some went right, leaving a gap down the middle which Going gratefully passed through. As he dived for the line Bennett tackled him head on and was half pushed to one side. As Bennett lay there Willie Duggan made a leap for Going but half missed and instead one of his boots caught his captain on the shoulder. Bennett was in agony for the rest of the game particularly after being very heavily tackled by Bryan Williams. He probably should have come off. His injury was later diagnosed as torn shoulder ligaments and a bruised chest. Even so, he managed to kick two penalties, one of 35 and one of 50 yards, to give the Lions a lead of 9–4.

Just before half-time the All Blacks loose head prop Brad Johnstone scored a dubious try following a penalty attempt by Bryan Williams. The right wing was aiming from the left touchline almost at the south pole which is directly behind the goal posts at the southerly end of Athletic Park. As the ball hung in front of the Lions posts the All Black forwards pelted up. Bill Osborne seemed to knock the ball over the line and Brad Johnstone fell on it. At first referee Peter Mc Davitt signalled a penalty to the Lions. Then, mysteriously, he changed his mind and indicated a try to the All Blacks. Williams's successful conversion made it 10–9 to the home side.

Once more though Bennett regained the lead for his team, this time with a simple 20-yard penalty kick. Two minutes later the Lions kissed the Test goodbye and, essentially, the series. Play was on their 10-yard line when Brynmor Williams, who was having his best game of the tour, broke to the open side and passed to Steve Fenwick. The centre moved the ball to flanker Trevor Evans outside him and there was a clear overlap for the Lions. Bennett was outside Evans and McGeechan and Irvine and Cobner outside their captain. The All Blacks had only two players to mark the attackers.

As it happened they needed only one. Bruce Robertson managed a half tackle on Evans, which was enough to dislodge his arm and the ball ballooned towards Bennett. With the opportunism for which he has become famous, the little red-headed Grant Batty grabbed the ball and scuttled fifty yards to score under the posts.

Before that the Lions were leading 12–10 and a try with a successful conversion would have made the score 18–10. Suddenly the 6 points had swung the other way and the Lions were trailing 12–16. 'The Batty try was a 12-point try,' Dawes said later.

In the second half the All Blacks faded. The urgency had gone. They didn't use the wind very well – stand off Duncan Robertson kicked too much and not very well. At the same time the resolve of the Lions stiffened considerably. Into the keen wind they salvaged some pride by preventing the All Blacks from scoring any more points. But the forward play was poor in both the tight and loose and they never got over losing the line outs three to one. Martin was outjumped by an inspired Andy Haden and New Zealand's back-of-the-line men Lawrie Knight and Ian Kirkpatrick combined to take out Willie Duggan where he had been so successful on tour and to win a lot of ball themselves. This was where Quinnell was missed most.

Afterwards the Lions felt slightly cheered at their second half performance. 'There was no way they were going to get through,' said Ian McGeechan. 'I feel happier going into the second Test with that behind us than I was for the first Test when we were still going into the unknown.' The more fanciful

Lions even described two of the All Blacks tries as lucky.

The All Blacks for their part, said had they played as well in the second half as in the first then the score would have been much higher. 'I feel the first Test is always the hardest to win for the home side,' said Jack Gleeson when he spoke to journalists in the subterranean dressing rooms at Athletic Park after the game. 'Now we have something to build on.' How right he was.

Chapter 10

Cobner's pack lead the revival

The groundwork for the Lions' revival, which began immediately after the first Test, was laid during four days spent in the coastal town of Timaru in South Island.

On the Sunday morning after their defeat the Lions awoke homesick and hungover. In Timaru the crisp and clear autumn air, the crackle of frost underfoot, the sight of the snow-capped Southern Alps in the distance eased their memories of the Test. Between Sunday and Thursday they found themselves a forward leader in Terry Cobner, who instilled some much-needed aggression into his men. Coincidentally, the management, so polite and courteous up to then, chose this week to flex their muscles too, with a blast about the standard of refereeing.

The result was that all of a sudden the tour came alight. The Lions were not going to be pushed around any more. The refereeing was bloody awful, and for once the management said so. The Lions started mixing and cheating as much as the laws and a New Zealand referee would let them get away with. 'To hell with everybody else!' they seemed to be saying. 'We are the only ones who matter.'

The process began on the Sunday evening when an impromptu sing-song in the bar of the team hotel turned into a spirited rendering by twenty or so Lions, who sat in a circle in one corner of the bar, leaving the hangers-on, the rugby groupies, in another. The symbolism of the circle was clear. Like frontiersmen in a Western, Lions were surrounded by outsiders and miles from home.

Outsiders entered the circle only by invitation as the Lions went through their repertoire: *The Leaving of Liverpool, Amazing*

Grace (singing just one word, 'Benny' their captain's nickname), *Flower of Scotland* and their favourite, *Last Thing on my Mind*. It was far and away the best sing-song of the tour. The tenseness almost visibly disappeared and those on the periphery could feel the tightening of the team spirit.

The healing continued at training the next morning when the Lions split, with John Dawes taking the the backs and Terry Cobner, the balding captain of Pontypool, the forwards. Cobner immediately began work on the line out and it was clear from what he was saying that he wanted his forwards to take the game to the New Zealanders. He wanted them to jump across the line out, to contest possession at every opportunity. He wanted the jumper supported and blocked so that the opposing forwards could not race through on to the scrum half, as had been happening before.

'We haven't been aggressive enough,' said Cobner as he sat on his bed after a late-afternoon shower. 'We have tended to think that when we get out there it will all come right. If the ball didn't go straight in the line out we tended to blame the wind. If it's our throw in, we *must* get the ball.'

The appointment of Cobner as captain for the Wednesday game against South and mid-Canterbury and North Otago was significant. He had been made captain for the sixth game of the tour but had had to leave the field after eight minutes with a split lip and cheek, and last Saturday's Test had been his first game since then. Clearly though, the Lions felt that it was his commitment to hard forward play that was needed. Not for nothing had he led Pontypool for eight successive seasons and built them into one of the hardest forward teams in Wales.

Equally important, though, was the team meeting on Tuesday evening, the night before the game. This was no ordinary meeting such as was held before each game with the management and all the players present. George Burrell and Dawes did not attend. It was just the fifteen men of the team and the replacements. For five minutes or so, Cobner laid down the law, spitting the words out, waving his hand around as he does in normal conversation. He told them a few home truths and generally said, as another Lion put it, 'just what we all felt needed to be said'. He asked for commitment and hardness.

The next day he got it. There was no reason before the game

why the Lions should have been expected to win by 39 points. For almost the first time in a provincial game they faced forwards who were taller than they were at the line outs, yet they won this phase of play by three to one; their scrummaging was venomous. And they blithely shrugged off some most peculiar refereeing decisions.

At one point a home forward went out of his way to stamp on Derek Quinnell when the Lion was on the ground a yard or so from a ruck. The referee's whistle peeped but it was a penalty against Quinnell he blew for, not one against the local player.

After playing slightly uphill in the first half, and nevertheless going into a narrow lead of 6–3 at half-time, the Lions went to work in the second half. They scored three tries in eleven minutes, paused and then wound up the game with three more tries this time in ten minutes. Andy Irvine converted them all, one being his own, a brilliant solo effort for which he ran through almost the whole home side. As he dotted the ball down there was a moment of stunned silence, as if nobody could believe what had happened and then everyone burst into spontaneous applause as a tribute to the most brilliant individual try of the tour. The Lions won 45–6.

The result of his success in that game was that Cobner had earned himself the pack leadership in every game in which he played from then on, which was a credit to him but also an indictment of the management for taking so long to recognize the talents of one man. Until the first Test the pack leadership had been handed around like pass the parcel and the result was that confusion was sown instead of confidence and discipline being bred. Cobner also joined the selection committee of Burrell, Dawes and Bennett.

Some of the team's resolution and commitment must have got through to the manager George Burrell for after the game he forsook the usual diplomatic platitudes that he and Dawes had been using up to that time. Burrell weighed into New Zealand referees for allowing the home sides to delay getting down for scrums and thus to avoid being pressurized by the more powerful Lions forwards. 'It is a point of law that teams must not delay in going down for scrums,' said Burrell, himself a former international referee. 'Even when we get down we have to retreat and it is a decided disadvantage to us to have to come back. If the referee decides this delaying is wilful then he should award a penalty to the Lions.'

Dawes followed his manager into battle. The coach was unhappy about the standard of refereeing and he called for far greater observation of the laws concerning offside at mauls and line outs. It was Dawes's opinion that the standard of refereeing spoilt the first half. 'Because we gained possession in the second half we were able to make a game of it,' said Dawes.

The reaction was predictable. The *Christchurch Star*, the evening paper in that town, led the front page the next day with a rebuttal of the Lions' criticisms by Len Kirk, once one of New Zealand's leading referees, who claimed that the Lions were deliberately breaking the laws.

Strangely the business of two sides slanging each other in public was far less sordid than usual. It seemed to clear the air in fact, and perhaps the resolution by the Lions' management would come to be regarded as significant too. So the Lions flew to Christchurch and their match with Canterbury on the Saturday with renewed vigour. As they began the second half of their fourteen-week tour some of the obvious errors had been put right and a new spirit had been kindled. Waiting for them at Lancaster Park were men who were determined to test that spirit.

In recent years there has not been much love lost between Canterbury and the British Lions. In 1966 Scotsman Jim Telfer gave a tongue-lashing to the home side at the after-match function. Five years later a record 53 000 spectators watched a brutal bloody encounter that even had spectators shivering with fear in their comfortable seats. The Lions lost their two best prop forwards that day – Ray McLoughlin with a thumb broken in hitting an opponent and Sandy Carmichael with extensive eye injuries. Later, they both went home.

What would happen this time? Former All Black Alex Wyllie, captaining Canterbury, his province, for the 70th time and playing his 168th game, wanted peace and so did everyone else. 'We will be hunting the ball and that is all,' said the time coach Stan (Tiny) Hill. 'There is no animosity, no thought of revenge,' said John Dawes.

One of the largest grounds in New Zealand, Lancaster Park, Christchurch, is dwarfed by a gasometer and a belching steel works, overlooked by a rococo Roman Catholic cathedral. It is a cavern without a soul. As the Lions' strongest available team took the field they knew the omens were against them. Under Grizz Wyllie's leadership, Canterbury had beaten Scotland, Ireland and England in the previous four years. The question was: would the introduction of the Welsh tip the balance to the Lions?

As it happened it was a flash of genius by Scotsman Andy Irvine which saved them. It was not a convincing victory to be sure. There were never more than 4 points between the two teams and the narrowness of the final margin is an accurate reflection of a clean, hard game in which the lead changed hands six times and not a single punch was thrown.

Cobner's influence was most marked. He switched the emphasis from the three quarters to the back row, tightening play up as one had suspected he would. He used the Lions' back row of himself, Trevor Evans and Willie Duggan to drive at Canterbury and thus tie down Canterbury's loose forwards and prevent them driving at the Lions' vulnerable midfield. They worked one such move just before half-time and a try then would have set them up for a convincing victory. But a fine tackle by Randall Scott on Gareth Evans just toppled the wing into touch after Cobner, Cotton, Brown and Martin had all handled in a thirty-yard surge to the Canterbury line.

It was a good first half for the Lions and they led 7–3. Canterbury had played a rather sterile and dated game based around Wyllie. Turgid stuff it was to be frank and the Lions dealt with it easily enough, though Wyllie tried everything he knew to confuse the visitors including wearing a jersey with No. 6 on it and packing down, in the main, at No. 8.

Gordon Brown, his already slightly misshapen left shoulder making him look more like Quasimodo than ever, sharpened up the line out and with Martin jumping at 4 the Lions outplayed Higginson and Vance Stewart. Yet still the doves fluttered unnecessarily in the dovecote, as twice stand off John Bevan fumbled the ball early on, as Doug Morgan had a wretched afternoon, as Andy Irvine had a clearance kick charged down. Again the Lions conceded too many penalties in the line out.

After half-time came Canterbury's revival. Wyllie's men took command at the line out, which enabled them to mount those peels and surges forward that forced the Lions forwards to turn and run backwards and ruck from positions of weakness. There seemed to be holes opening up everywhere in front of Canterbury players as they won good ball from these rucks. Their All Black half backs Lyn Davis and Doug Bruce dovetailed beautifully in tune but the centres were badly out of touch.

Even so Canterbury scored two tries in fourteen minutes which was enough for them to take and keep the lead even after J.J. Williams had gone over for a cheeky try set up by Willie Duggan. The Lions' No. 8 had noticed that there would be a gap on the side of the scrum after Wyllie had gone off with an injured leg and before his replacement could come on. As the Lions heeled Duggan picked up and flicked Williams an easy pass. The game moved into injury time with the score 13–11 to the home side.

Then came the turning point. The Lions were awarded a penalty in their own 25 and Cobner told them to run it. With a surprising turn of speed for such a stocky fellow – he is 5ft 8in and 12½ stone – John Bevan made a slashing break of forty yards and then passed to the accelerating Irvine outside him. Irvine nearly dropped the ball but he was going so fast he outpaced all but two Cantabrians covering across.

The entire stand stood as the dark-haired Scotsman pelted for the corner. Surely, they thought, he couldn't score from seventy-five yards? And he could not, Wyllie's replacement Stewart Purdon just getting him into touch five yards from glory. But from the line out came a scrum and at that Scott Cartwright was inexcusably caught offside under his own posts. Irvine's kick was a formality for a man in such regal all-round form.

So the Lions won their twelfth game and confirmed their revival. They were lucky that Doug Heffernan, the Canterbury full back, missed eight kicks at goal (five out of six penalties in the first half). But they needed luck for once. They sniffed the air, went for a sauna and massage and, as they moved on, they concluded it wouldn't be so bad to come back to Christchurch in two weeks for the second Test after all.

Chapter 11

Ian McGeechan goes to school

The classroom was full of boys, some in short trousers, some in long. Aged between 13 and 18, they wore light grey trousers, sweaters and open-neck shirts. The metal-framed wooden desks had been pushed back against the walls so that extra chairs could be brought in, and the white walls were dotted with maps and posters of Japan. Outside the window other pupils bustled past, their heads down against the wind, their books tucked firmly under their arms.

In front of the blackboard stood Ian McGeechan looking strangely formal in his blazer and flannels, his dark hair curling down over his blazer collar. It was 2.15 on a wet, blustery afternoon in June in what could have been the first class after lunch at Fir Tree Middle School in Moortown, Leeds, the comprehensive school where McGeechan teaches.

In fact it was Buller High School, Westport in South Island, the only town on the west coast that the Lions were to stay at during their tour. Ian McGeechan was visiting the school that had adopted him. In return for his visit he would later receive a handsome scrapbook the pupils had filled with press cuttings and photographs from the tour.

The idea of rugby players visiting New Zealand being adopted by schools was started in 1956 by John Sinclair of Palmerston North. Now it has spread to South Africa and Britain. Sinclair gave some clippings to a South African when they were touring New Zealand in 1956 and he put together a scrapbook for the father of one of the other Springboks. He also paired off thirty-two boys from Palmerston North Boys High School with Springbok players.

In 1965 the first and second fifteens at Palmerston North Boys H S each adopted one of the visiting South Africans and the boys wrapped and sent back to South Africa 164 parcels of presents for the tourists. The following year when the British Lions toured, Sinclair had expanded the scheme to thirty-two schools, each of them taking one Lion.

By 1977 then, the scheme was so advanced that the Lions all knew before reaching Richmond which was their school. Tradition demanded that the captain, Phil Bennett, should go to Palmerston North Boys H S. He had, like the rest of the team, had a letter from the Four Home Unions long before left home encouraging him to make contact with his school at the earliest possible opportunity. McGeechan wrote to Buller within a few days of arriving in New Zealand and almost by return he received from the school a brochure about Westport.

Most of the schools that participated in the scheme were those that had been in it from the start. They were both public and state schools, as well as boys only and mixed schools. Gordon Brown was adopted by the same school as had adopted him in 1971 – Kings High School, Dunedin.

'The idea is great for us,' says McGeechan. 'In South Africa with the Lions in 1974 I got a scrapbook for every Test and one for all the provincial games. That way you have a permanent record, the sort of thing you will treasure for the rest of your life. And let's face it, you don't have time on tour to do one yourself.'

In return the Lions were expected to visit their school on one afternoon. Often they went in groups of three to help each other out. What they did at the school depended on the master in charge. Gordon Brown first spoke for a half-hour to thirty-six of the school's better rugby players and then addressed the whole school and staff. Derek Quinnell gave a rugby clinic and did some specific coaching with the pupils of his school, Pukekohe High School, in Pukekohe, twenty miles south of Auckland.

Early in the tour several Lions reported they had been put in front of the school assembly – as many as 1000 pupils – and asked to speak for ten or fifteen minutes. George Burrell had to do this at Hastings Boys High School and he found it a little nerve-wracking. He circulated a letter to all headmasters saying he did not want the Lions to talk in front of large gatherings unless they didn't mind doing so. He would prefer, he said, that they addressed small groups and answered questions.

The essence of the scheme, though, was cooperation and for the Lions to put in as much work as they could. 'The scheme is only as good as the Lion makes it,' points out Sinclair. 'The Lion turns the key.'

McGeechan turned his key well. He, Bruce Hay, the Scottish full back, and scrum half Douglas Morgan, another Scot, all visited Buller High School together. After being picked up from their hotel by Norman Crawshaw, the vice-principal of the school, they stood in front of the class and invited questions. 'I always like to break the ice,' McGeechan said later. 'I like to try and make them laugh early so they will relax and ask the questions they want to ask and not the ones they feel they should ask.'

'Perhaps I should introduce myself by saying a little about how I got here,' said McGeechan. 'I started playing club rugby when I was still at school in 1964. I had my first trial for Scotland four years later but the Scottish selectors decided they could do without me for another four years. Then in 1972 I was selected to play for Scotland against Ian Kirkpatrick's All Blacks.

'I have now got twenty-four caps, which I am very pleased about and in my second season for Scotland I was lucky enough to be picked to play for the Lions in South Africa. Now we have been selected to come here for three and a half months, which certainly beats working.' Slowly the children were warming to McGeechan and this last remark brought a round of titters.

'When I am at home,' McGeechan continued, 'I try and teach. The other staff members say that I am not there very often. Let me introduce my two friends.'

'Bruce here, known as Ken to his friends, is an electrician at a colliery. And Dougie is a chiropodist. Who knows what a chiropodist is?' he asked, pronouncing the word with a soft *c*. There was a pause.

'A foot specialist,' said a boy from the back.

'That's right,' said McGeechan. 'Well done. Now perhaps you would like to ask us some questions?'

A tall, thin-faced boy put his hand up. 'Will you win the Test series?' he asked.

'I feel much better about the second Test now than I did

before the first Test,' replied McGeechan. He didn't elaborate and there was another pause.

'No one else got any questions?' he asked, looking around the room. 'Well who is going to back West Coast-Buller against the Lions on Wednesday afternoon?' There was a longer, louder round of laughter.

Doug Morgan stepped forward. He hadn't said anything up to now. 'Most of you have seen our games on television,' he said.

McGeechan, sensing he could get a laugh, added quickly, 'What do you think of them so far?'

'Rubbish,' was the answer, chanted loudly by half the class and the Lions laughed as much as anybody.

'How much training do you do?' asked a small boy near the front of the class.

'I didn't play at all in April,' McGeechan replied. 'My training schedule started one week before I came away. I was pretty fit anyway, after a full season and I didn't want to get too fit too soon in the tour.' He paused. 'But don't tell John Dawes that' he added.

'Do you get paid for going on tour with the Lions?'

'I get pocket money. In South Africa it was 75 pence per day but out here we have been given a rise and we get £3 each day or N Z $38.50 each week.

'When I am gallivanting around the world,' said Morgan, 'I am lucky because my wife comes and covers for me.'

'I am the same,' said Bruce Hay. 'My boss is very good to me and I am being looked after while I am away, too.'

The class had loosened up now and the questions they had been preparing for weeks were coming faster. Morgan and Hay, seemingly sensing the class relaxing, joined in more too.

'Which island plays better rugby?' asked one boy. 'It must be the South Island.'

McGeechan made a diplomatic reply. 'It is different in each island.'

'What New Zealand players have impressed you most?'

'There was a centre or second five-eighth, as you would call him, who played for Southland. He was a natural player.' McGeechan spoke with some feeling because he had to mark the youngster. 'What was his name?'

The class quickly supplied the answer. 'Pokere,' they said.

'Bruce Robertson has also impressed me. And I think that Doug has found very few poor half backs.'

'Do you know who broke your arm?' someone asked Bruce Hay, remembering that the full back had broken his arm playing for Scotland against New Zealand at Eden Park, Auckland in 1975.

'Yes I know,' replied the full back and the class laughed.

'I didn't realize it for some time after it happened. I dropped the ball and I was so cross with myself for doing that it was some minutes before I realized my arm was hurting. The first time you play for your country is so nerve-wracking you can hardly remember anything afterwards. I just remember that I didn't want to come off in case it proved to be nothing.'

The questions were becoming more specialized now. Hay was asked who was the best full back he had seen on tour.

'Doug Heffernan had a very good game for New Zealand Universities against us,' he replied. 'But, you know, so much of full-back play depends on whether you are going forwards or backwards. If you are going forward you can be made to look very good. But if you are going backward it is very different.'

'Do you think the Lions were conned into playing a running game by the way the Blacks selected Colin Farrell, a running full back, and then played a tight game in the Test?'

'A Test match is a different match altogether,' replied McGeechan. 'You are putting a Lions jersey on for the sixth or seventh time. You've got to remind yourself that it is not just another game. It is up to the individual to say to himself, "This is a Test match. This is different." We didn't train at all on the Friday before the match because we felt that we wanted more time to think about the game. It didn't work out that way and we made a lot of mistakes in the first twenty minutes.'

'Basically,' added Morgan. 'We are playing twenty-five internationals in three and a half months. The players we meet have got eighty minutes in which to sell themselves. It is the game of a lifetime for most of them and they will never play against another Lions side. It is their only chance to impress the selectors.'

The shyness and diffidence among the schoolchildren had gone. They were lining up, putting their hands up and tending to start their questions at the same time so the Lions had to point to the questioner they wanted to hear from next.

'Wasn't there some bad refereeing in the game against the Universities?' asked a little boy in glasses sitting in the front row, referring to the game on the Tuesday before the first Test when the Lions were beaten 21–9.

McGeechan was ready for this one. He had captained the Lions that day and had given that question and the match a lot of thought. 'We ought to have played better,' he said thoughtfully and candidly. 'With the best referee in the world we would have lost that day. We ought to be big enough to take that defeat.' There was a pause as the implication of what McGeechan had said sank in. In another, older, more mature audience, there might have been a spontaneous round of applause.

'How good a captain is Tane Norton?'

'He's good,' replied McGeechan.

'What impressed me about him last Saturday in the Canterbury game,' added Morgan, 'was that he never said a word in the whole game until Alex Wyllie the Canterbury captain went off. That was very disciplined of him and probably as the All Black captain, very hard for him to do.'

'What is the best place you have visited in New Zealand?'

'Westport,' said McGeechan quickly, amidst laughter.

It was nearly 3.15 now and Norman Crawshaw was showing signs of wanting to bring the class to an end. 'Do you have any advice for the boys going off to Australia on a two-week tour soon?' he asked. 'They play six games in two weeks.'

'Get plenty of sleep,' said McGeechan, and the class hooted derisively.

'Eat only what you like,' said Bruce Hay. 'Don't pay any attention to anything that might sound exotic unless you have a very strong tummy.'

Crawshaw stepped forward and presented the three Lions with a tie that had a cross between a Lion and a whitebait as its motif.

McGeechan reached back into a small case he had brought with him.

'Is the First X V captain here?' he asked, and a tall, slim boy from near the back of the class got up and went forward. McGeechan presented him with a pair of socks from Headingley and a Headingley club tie.

Who said he could only kick and chase? J.J. Williams's brilliant try in the second Test.

Waking up was easier the next morning when J.J. read the good news of a Test victory.

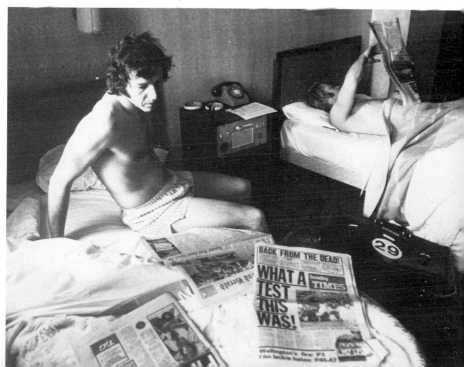

Split lip or no, Cobner's message was clear at half-time in the second Test.

He may be old, he may be bald, but the Lions were delighted when Sid Going was dropped for the third Test.

Ian Kirkpatrick, left, and Graham Price exchanged words
and fists at least once.

Are they both on the same side? In the mud sometimes
even team-mates couldn't distinguish one another.

You can have plaice and chips, fish and chips or egg and chips. Make your mind up, Cob.

At Gaelic football Moss Keane was unequalled. At volleyball he was a graceful mover.

Clive Williams can swim but he made Allan Martin give him a lift in the pool at Christchurch all the same.

It's not Irish noughts and crosses Phil Orr is playing. He is working out room pairings for the next hotel.

The captain of the First X V replied, 'On behalf of the rest of the team I would like to thank you for coming and to wish you all the best on the rest of your tour.'

But McGeechan hadn't finished. 'Is the captain of the sixth-grade team here?' he asked. 'You might like to wear that sometime,' he said, handing him another Headingley tie. He turned to Norman Crawshaw. 'For the First X V here are fifteen Lions badges. I've got some smaller T-shirts for the younger boys which you might enjoy training in. I have also left some more ties so the best players on the Australian tour might be presented with them perhaps.'

Crawshaw received the badges with pride and thanked McGeechan, Morgan and Hay for coming. He took them into the staff room for tea.

'The boys will be talking among themselves now about the questions they wanted to ask and then forgot,' he said, as if apologizing to McGeechan for the shortage of questions at the beginning.

'Not at all,' said McGeechan politely, stirring his tea. 'They were very good. A little more outspoken than the boys at home perhaps.'

He looked around the staff room, at the notices on the walls, the worn, yet comfortable chairs, the big wireless in the corner, the pigeon holes for each member of the staff and the big solid central table. 'Staff rooms don't change much the world over, do they?'

Some weeks after he got back to Leeds, he received his scrapbook. Buller High School had done him proud. The best scrapbook of all however, was Douglas Morgan's, prepared for him by the pupils of Rosehill College, Papakura, a mixed state school near Auckland. It measured 2½ feet by 1 foot, was 2 inches thick and bound with a nut and screw, and weighed a couple of pounds. A committee of thirty had laboured lovingly over it for weeks. Inside were press cuttings from New Zealand and British papers, as well as seven or eight original photographs taken of Morgan while playing.

On Sunday morning 14 August, three boys, three girls and the master in charge of the project arrived at the Royal International hotel in Auckland and presented it to Morgan.

Chapter 12

Seven days with Doug Morgan

For a week midway through the tour Douglas Morgan sat down once each day and recorded his day's activities and comments into a tape recorder. This is his account of seven of the hundred days he spent in New Zealand with the 1977 British Lions. It begins on Monday 4 July, two days after the Lions had beaten Wellington 13–6 and ends the day after the Lions' victory at Christchurch in the second Test.

Monday 4 July

Monday morning would generally be a nine o'clock breakfast before a hard training session, but today was different. We should have left Wellington yesterday but high winds virtually closed the airport so we didn't even leave the hotel. We were told that we would be training on Monday morning and would fly on to Blenheim in the South Island some time during the day. At nine o'clock this morning we heard that Wellington airport was closed and that we were to be put on a bus and driven to Palmerston North where the airport was open. First we had our usual Monday morning team meeting. This one lasted for a half-hour, which was quite long because we touched on all the points we felt we had to discuss before the Test match. Generally we try and leave rugby from the Saturday night until Monday morning. Though everything is fresh in your mind on Saturday evening it is an unwritten law that rugby is not spoken about after six in the evening. Then we went by coach to the airport, stopping off for sandwiches, coffee, tea and biscuits on the way. Had we been scheduled to travel by coach we would have trained first and then travelled in which case we might have had some beer with us. But we were to train at Blenheim after our journey so we didn't drink on the way. It is possible to play cards on a coach but depending on the time of day a lot of the boys like to sleep.

Gordon Brown has a cassette recorder and that is generally playing. Personally I like to stay awake during the day unless I am very tired. We had an accident about an hour out of Wellington when the coach ran into the back of a car that wanted to turn right. A girl was driving it and she was hysterical but she wasn't injured in any way other than she had a whiplash to her neck. From Palmerston North we flew in a Fokker Friendship to Blenheim. When we took off the plane was wobbling a bit and I think most of them thought that it was the worst flight of the tour so far. About 300 feet off the ground it was really bad, according to Geech [Ian McGeechan] our internal pilot. Geech tells us when the flaps are coming down and what we should be doing and what we shouldn't be doing. I think that Bobby Windsor is the worst flier in the party. Willie Duggan is not very good and says he will never fly again after he gets back to Dublin.

Once we arrived at Blenheim airport we went straight to the ground and trained there for forty-five minutes. It is a very nice ground, firm, and one of the few they have actually made an effort to look after because prior to our game they had moved the last two Saturday games. We had our training gear with us in our blue Adidas bags. The rest of our baggage went separately and was looked after by Doc Murdoch.

We came straight to our hotel [the D B Grosvenor in Blenheim] after training and I got myself organized. It was my turn to have a room to myself. There are thirty players in the party. The captain always gets a single room so that leaves twenty-nine, which means fourteen double rooms and one single. Phil Orr and Terry Cobner have a list of rooms and who has shared with whom. To prevent cliques they try and work it out that no one shares with same person twice on tour, though this is not always possible. The team is picked on the morning after a game and told to us. Then Phil and Terry get together and work out the room pairings.

This room is typical of the ones we have had on tour, though it would be a little smaller than most. It has two beds, a colour television, cupboard, radio, telephone by the bedside and in the adjoining bathroom a shower/bath and a lavatory. I am lucky here because none of the other boys has a television in their room. Generally we have had a black-and-white set. Personally I prefer a bath, especially on a trip like this when you are training every day and you get knocks and bruises. I find it helps ease the aches and pains.

After we got to the hotel I had a lie down for a couple of hours and then went down to dinner about seven. Most days we are only allowed to have the set menu but because we hadn't had a proper lunch we were allowed to go à la carte last night. I had shrimp cocktail, fish, roast pork. Early in the tour we had a team meeting and complained about the food, which hadn't been very good. From then on we were allowed to have à la carte on match nights each week.

We can only have soft drinks with our meals, not beer, unless we want to pay for it ourselves. On match nights we are allowed wine with our meals and usually only one bottle between four. We are limited to New Zealand wine. If we want Australian, French or German wines then we have to pay the difference between the most expensive New Zealand wine and the wine we want.

After dinner, Andy Irvine, Ian McGeechan and I went across the road to the local Retired Servicemen's Association hall for a quiet game of snooker and pool. I went to bed about quarter to ten. I am an early bedder back home and before a match out here I go to bed about ten or quarter past. I might read a little but generally I fall asleep within minutes.

Tuesday 5 July

Breakfast in bed in my room. I do this on match day mornings. I slept well and was woken by the waitress bringing in the tea, toast and cornflakes at 9.15. At 11.15 we had the team meeting we always have on the day of the match. It lasted only five or ten minutes and then we went straight down for lunch. I have an omelette and an egg, sherry and milk nog for lunch on match days. I find it filling and I get plenty of glucose. After lunch there was an hour to fill so I cleaned my boots, laid my kit out

and relaxed. I always put my boots into my bag last. I check my
kit two or three times in the hour while I am waiting. I take
boots, socks, shorts, underpants – no jockstrap – shirt. I don't
wear a mouthguard. I usually take some shampoo though Doc
generally has some as well.

Until recently we had to supply our own laces but now Doc
has a supply that will last us for the rest of the tour. I find that I
don't get through laces very quickly. I generally pack one spare
pair of boots in case anything goes wrong – in case a boot splits,
for instance. I also pack a tube of deep heat – Capsolin. It is very
hot and I use it if I have had a bump. I keep a track suit in my bag
as well.

Normally we always sing on our journey to the ground but
this one was so short that we had hardly any time. We managed
Flower of Scotland, Last Thing on my Mind and then Gordon
Brown, who is the choirmaster, led us in chanting: 'Give me an
L, give me an I, give me an O,' etc. We try and sit in special
pairings on the bus – the props together, the half backs, the
centres.

Into the dressing room. If there is still forty-five minutes to
go before kick-off then there is a lot of chattering going on but
with a half hour to go everyone has withdrawn into themselves.
John Bevan and Ian McGeechan give their boots a final polish.
Fifteen minutes before kick-off the captain of the day says a few
words and puts us through our final warm-up. Everybody has to
be changed by that time, with boots tied and having had their
rub from Doc Murdoch if necessary. There was no room today
in the dressing room for Doc to put up his masseur's table so we
weren't able to have a last-minute rub.

In the game we started off very slowly as we generally do and
Marlborough Nelson Bays started as every other side have.
They went completely berserk in the opening twenty minutes
and in that time all we could do was sum them up and see if there
were any weaknesses. I must say I was surprised by how well
they handled the ball. The little we had heard of them suggested
it was going to be an easy game. But in fact, we only won 40–23.
They scored more points against us than any other team. I was
happy with the way I played. The first pass was in front of John
Bevan and he didn't quite get to it but as far as I'm concerned as
long as I put the ball in front of my stand off I am happy with

that. I like to get a good kick in early on. From a scrum in the middle of the field I sent a kick into the corner and into touch. That set me up for the rest of the game. Twenty minutes after the game started I pulled a muscle in my leg and it gradually got tighter and tighter. When I took that conversion attempt in the second half I was trying to protect my leg more than anything. I didn't really follow through and I jarred my leg, which was a mistake. So I came off and immediately wrapped a towel around some ice, put it on the muscle and held it there for twenty minutes. Brynmor came on for me. Then I had a shower and got changed. The changing room was fairly cramped and that is one thing that is not comparable over here with the facilities back home. For a country of New Zealand's standing the changing facilities are poor. Wellington is dreadful. There are wee showers and only one small toilet. You also have to pee in the shower I suppose.

Then we had the usual after-match function with the two teams and officials. The food was very good this time, sandwiches, cakes, hot pies and sausages. I am not a great eater after a game. I prefer to have a couple of beers and eat later on. After the after-match function we went straight back to the hotel and into the team room. Last night a sing-song didn't develop because we didn't have very long before dinner. It is compulsory to be in the team room after games and if you are not or if you are late then the penalty is generally a glass of beer down in one and if you are very late maybe two glasses. With the type of beer out here it pays to be on time. After dinner it was a pretty heavy scene in the hotel so Geech and I went to try and play snooker but it was too busy, so we came back and played cards in the team room until going to bed at 11.30.

Those heavies that come out from Britain I suppose do have a certain right to come up and talk to us and I don't mind talking to them at all. The trouble is that a large percentage of heavies go over the score. Some of the things they say are just silly and naive. For example in Wellington the night after the Westport game one got hold of Dave Burcher and myself after we had been out for a meal. Westport was very wet and muddy, you remember. This idiot was saying to us, 'It must have been a bit damp yesterday.'

'Dave and I were in the mood for a bit of fun so we said, 'No, not at all, it was bone dry, a perfect pitch.' We kept the conversation going for about ten minutes and then left him. He still didn't know how bad the conditions had been.

Wednesday 6 July

We met in the team room about 9.30 and Dod [manager George Burrell] announced the team for the Test match. It was all rather unemotional. Those boys that were in for the first time were congratulated and there were commiserations for those who had been left out. I didn't really think I had any chance of being picked because of the rib injury I had had. When Brynmor was injured I was forced to play sooner than I wanted to after my own injury and because of that I made mistakes I wouldn't normally have made. Initially I was disappointed I wasn't picked for the first Test but having seen Brynmor and Phil Bennett play together so well in the first Test I understood why they were kept together.

I thought at first it was all going to be too quick for Bryn. He was rushing around and I told him to settle down and play his normal game. When I watch him I notice both his strengths and his weaknesses, his weaknesses more than his strengths. I am sure he does the same when he watches me. He likes to spin pass a lot and to spin pass it all the time you have to have a certain amount of wind up. In picking the ball from the scrum and getting it away you can sometimes catch the ball with your elbow. I would not say it is slow but there is a time in the movement as he goes back on his backswing when his arm has gone back towards the opposition and therefore he is vulnerable to being disrupted. I believe that as far as the stand off is concerned he wants the ball in his hands as quickly as possible and it doesn't really matter how far it goes so long as it is in front of him quickly.

I only did some very light training this morning. I did 100 press ups and the same number of sit ups but I wanted to favour my leg and not strain it so I didn't do any running.

We flew on to Christchurch after an early lunch. It was a very short, smooth flight. After checking into our hotel in Christchurch, about ten of us went to physio. While we were sitting there waiting the door opened and All Black skipper Tane

Norton came in. He said he wondered whether the rumours he had heard about us all going to physio were true. He talked to Bobby Windsor a lot and then he disappeared through into the consulting rooms and there were cracks about him getting preferential treatment because he was captain of the All Blacks.

He came back out two minutes later with a skeleton and held it up and said, 'I've just got a new spine and pelvis for Saturday.'

I called my wife Doreen in Edinburgh last night only to discover that she was on holiday. I have phoned twice so far on this trip. I don't like doing it because sometimes Doreen gets a bit upset. But she hadn't been too well and in a recent letter she said she was depressed. We have one child, Mandy, who is five. Like me Doreen is a chiropodist but whereas I have my own practice she does domiciliary visiting, that is to say she goes out to visit old age pensioners who can't get to clinics.

After that abortive phone call I watched the previous day's game on television. The quality of commentating and production over here is very poor by comparison with back home. The commentary lacks atmosphere. I thought that the first try they scored was great but in the commentary it was 'such and such got the ball and such and such went over the line' and that was basically it. I don't find there is much difference in watching on television a game I have played in. What it showed though, was how much their backs lay up offside.

Apart from going away on school trips and other rugby tours this is the first time in my life I have ever had to share a room with another fellow. I don't have problems at all. People say that Gordon Brown is a big snorer but I have had no trouble with him. The worst one I have come across so far is Steve Fenwick. It's not so much a snore with him, more a high-pitched squeal. I've shared with Willie Duggan and he's a bit of a snorer. For this week they have put Fran Cotton in with Gordon Brown because Fran can sleep in any conditions. He is called King Kipper.

I don't unpack my suitcase very often. I just keep the things I need most at the top and work down from there. And the laundry is so good, coming back the day you send it, that there is no problem with washing. I send almost everything to the laundry. The only things I don't send are my Lions sweaters and polo neck jumpers because there is a chance they may go missing. A couple of sweaters have been damaged already by people trying to take the badges off.

Thursday 7 July

We had a team meeting at 9.30 in our kit because we were going to train just across the road in Hagley Park. We warmed up for a half hour and then the backs and the forwards split up. I did it all. I couldn't run flat out but at least I could run. I went with the forwards and they did a half-hour's scrummaging, twenty minutes' line-out work and then everybody came together for a quarter of an hour's unopposed rugby. Training up until the first Test was becoming very predictable but since then John Dawes has introduced things that we did at the beginning of the tour, a bit of competitive stuff, three against one with the ball, two people trying to wrestle the ball from one person. The day before a game we would train for a half-hour or forty minutes, no more. Today it was an hour and three quarters because we are not training tomorrow.

After lunch the boys went to a warehouse in town to buy some jeans and denim shirts. We were offered them wholesale, which meant about fourteen dollars. I couldn't buy any because I always have trouble with my thighs. I have a fairly small waist and a big bum and I couldn't get any to fit me.

Thursday night we had a compulsory film show for the team and subs in the team room of the hotel. It was *The Duchess and the Dirtwater Fox* and it was quite funny. About ten o'clock they brought in some coffee and sandwiches. That was the first time anything had been organized for the team on a Thursday night.

Friday 8 July

I had a long lie-in and a free morning. I got up at half-past ten. There was no mail for me this morning and I spent the morning tidying up. Mail has been reaching me fairly regularly, two or three letters at once. It is sent to me c/o the New Zealand R U in Wellington and they send it in big sacks or someone brings it up with them. The duty boy of the day hands it out. There was a bus trip out for the team immediately after lunch. We went to a working men's club where there was snooker, bowls, pool and we could be perfectly alone. The bus dropped us off at physio on the way back and after physio I caught a taxi back to the hotel. The NZRU pay for all the taxis we use to and from physio. There was another film at night and after that I went to bed and watched the Connors *v.* Borg Wimbledon final on television.

Saturday 9 July

Made myself a cup of tea around ten and got up for the team meeting at 11.15. Not much to say in this meeting because we all knew that we had to win this Test. Dod spoke first, then John and last Phil.

When we got to the ground we dropped our kit off and looked at the pitch. It looked a lot better than most of us had expected after all the rain, apart from the middle third. The dressing rooms at Lancaster Park are big and our room had a concrete floor covered with duckboards. They were well lit this time; last time, for the Universities game, the lights failed.

I was getting quite familiar with the dressing rooms now. This was the third time I had changed there so far on tour. For the Universities game I used the same changing peg as I had when Scotland played Canterbury two years ago. We lost both games. For the Canterbury game this time I moved to a new peg, next to Willie Duggan. We won that game so I used the same peg for the Test.

We changed quickly and then the replacements went upstairs to the committee room and had a cup of tea so that the team could be left on their own. I wore my Lions kit and a track suit with a wet suit over my track suit. I had a blanket to wrap around me. You could sense the determination in the dressing room. People tended to wander about nervously, hands in pockets, looking at the floor.

Even just before a Test Steve Fenwick is the most talkative player. He has an incredible temperament for a game, for any game, very relaxed. Maybe he is bottling it all up but if there was any joke to crack he would crack it.

When we took our seats in the stand I was next to Bruce Hay. I don't think I will sit next to Bruce very often. He gets terribly nervous, covering himself with a blanket, twitching. Brynmor made a mess of the first ball as it came out of the scrum. He tried to kick it, changed his mind and got a raking for it. He started similarly in the first one or two games out here and was made to look wrong by the pace being too fast for him. He had a kick after fifteen or twenty minutes from just inside the 25 at a lineout that sent the All Blacks back to just inside their own half. That would have helped his confidence.

I don't remember what the score was at half-time, was it 13–3 or 13–6? I had expected the All Blacks to go off with a bigger bang. I could see that in the scrummaging and line out we were functioning particularly well in the first twenty minutes, by comparison with the first Test. I felt that we needed just one more score to make it safe yet even at the end I never felt that we were going to lose.

It looked a fairly dirty game to me and, as our forwards said later, the All Blacks weren't too concerned where they put their feet. It was unnecessary. I think rough play always is but I think that the Blacks had got a helluva fright in the first twenty minutes and they tried to psyche us out of it by late tackling. No one talks about late tackling. It is pretty well left to one's self to look after one's self. You know what to do to someone who is late tackling you. I am not very emotional during a game. I just sit and watch it. What was happening on the field didn't anger me. David Burcher was sitting on the end of the row and he was pretty pent up but John Dawes was quiet. He doesn't make many comments during a game. He has very good vision for things like alignment of backs, backs lying offside at a ruck or maul.

As we walked back to the dressing room many people said well done to us. In the dressing room there was tea, lemonade and orange. No champagne. There was a doctor seeing about stitches. Everybody was very excited and yet we realized that there was still another five weeks to go. Dod and John came in and went around each individual and patted them on the back or shook their hand. Then we all went upstairs for the after-match function. I spoke to Lyn Davis and Grant Batty and Doug Bruce, and they thought that we had deserved to win.

Back in the hotel we went straight into the team room for a long sing-song and it was only then that it got through to many of us that we had actually won. There was some do on at a local club, Linwood, I think, but by the time we had had the sing-song and dinner it was too late. It was fairly lively down in the dining room I understand though I was late down because some of us stayed in the team room for a blether. After dinner it was everyone for himself. We spent some time around the bar and after ten o'clock the team room began functioning. I went up there around midnight and there were a few happy people sitting around talking and drinking. The bar downstairs was very small and once you got a few folk in there wasn't much room for others. The team room upstairs was that bit too big so you didn't really get an atmosphere going. Some people were dancing in the team room. I finally went to bed about two.

Sunday 10 July

Doc Murdoch came around and woke me up. He was wearing a fireman's helmet and he had an enormous bottle of Scotch and he insisted I had a Scotch. Then a sing-song started in Ian McGeechan's and Steve Fenwick's room, next to ours, and went on for two hours or so. I had two or three bottles of beer, packed my case and by 1.30 we were away to the airport for the flight to Auckland.

Gordon Brown was duty boy and he was pretty good at organizing everyone even though it is difficult on Sunday morning. We have to travel wearing either the red shirt or red polo neck with either the blazer or sweater as well. It was an ordinary scheduled flight and it was pretty quiet. People had a lot of sleep to catch up on after last night.

There was no mail waiting for me when I arrived in the hotel here but I didn't really expect any. Getting regular letters from my wife has helped me cope with the homesickness. Doreen and Lynda Hay, Bruce's wife, get together a lot. In fact, Lynda spent last week-end at our house. I don't worry about my business because it is fairly well established. It is shut three days each week and my wife handles it the other two days. I don't have anyone working with me, no partners.

When I left my wife was completely booked up for the two days she was working right until I return. Once I go back I reckon I will be fully booked a month or six weeks ahead. I am not worried that some of my regular customers will leave me while I am away. I think that if they have been satisfied with the treatment they had from me before I left then they will always come back. I also find it surprising how many people are interested in rugby, even old ladies. All they want to do is to chat to me about rugby.

I spent the rest of Sunday quietly around the hotel. Somebody asked me that evening what the difference was between this tour and our tour with Scotland. The answer is the difference is like night and day. The Scots were only here for five weeks and we found that we were accepted everywhere and welcomed with open arms. This tour people have been antagonistic to us. I like New Zealand very much. I find it is similar to Scotland, particularly down in the South Island around Invercargill and Christchurch. I wouldn't emigrate here but if I had to work here I wouldn't be averse to it.

Chapter 13

Jack Gleeson:
coach with honours

The British Lions first met the All Blacks coach Jack Gleeson in Masterton after they had easily beaten Wairarapa-Bush in their opening match. As a way of starting a twenty-five-match tour it was exemplary. Snow had fallen the previous night and it was only just above freezing at Memorial Park for the game. A piercing fifty-miles-an-hour wind from the Rimutaka Hills to the east whipped rain and sometimes sleet from one end of the pitch to the other. By half-time some Lions had lost control of their fingers.

Even so the Lions played running rugby from start to finish, opening with a try after three minutes and handling the ball at times as if it were a dry day. The backs ran in six tries; Terry Cobner, a forward, got two. 'The Lions did enough to be described as impressive,' admitted Brian Lochore, former No. 8 and All Black captain, at the aftermatch function. Laudatory words from such a great man but he had no reason to be other than truthful.

I moved over to Jack Gleeson and introduced myself. I found myself looking at a man of medium height, slight, with spiky, sandy-coloured hair that frizzed in all directions from his head. He had a cup of tea in his hand and he wore the overcoat and fawn scarf that were to become a familiar sight in months to come. He directed at me a keen gaze, his head slightly to one side. There were aquiline features in his face suggesting a Mediterranean heritage, yet the colour of his hair and his name clearly indicated an Irish background.

'What did you think of that?' I asked after the initial courtesies were over. 'You must remember that Wairarapa-Bush aren't a very good side at present,' he pointed out. He was stinting almost to the point of caution. He was also honest and realistic.

So that was Jack Gleeson – cautious, honest and realistic. In weeks to come as I got to know him better I realized that he was pragmatic and friendly, too. He would talk to anyone, but if he wasn't ready then they had to wait.

Scratch away at the soil of middle New Zealand and you would unearth Jack Gleeson – hard-working, of British ancestry, father of two children, a sports enthusiast, a reactionary. In short, a good solid Kiwi. Gleeson is a middle-of-the-road New Zealander. 'Worship the mean, cultivate the mediocre,' wrote New Zealand's M.K. Joseph of his countrymen and Gleeson certainly seems to allow himself precious little regard for the out-of-the-ordinary.

He is a Catholic with a broad puritanical streak and has laid down ground rules for his wife and two children. 'I am not particularly religious but I do believe in making sacrifices, in determining right from wrong. I believe in the Ten Commandments.'

He does not smoke and he drinks moderately. In conversation you almost have to strain to hear him on occasions and outwardly he seems to be no more excited by victory than he is obviously disappointed by defeat. He chooses smart clothes, allowing himself to be modish to the extent of wearing suits with flared trousers, yet eschewing bright colours. And he votes National Party, which means Conservative.

'I vote National Party because I consider that their consideration for me as a businessman is better than Labour,' he says. 'Our harder times have always been when Labour is in, whereas with the National Party there seems to be plenty for all. If the worker is getting plenty, well, so does the businessman. I feel that Labour's views over the last few years have been more of state control and I am a private enterprise man. My business is private. I am not controlled by anyone. The less we have of state control and monopolies the better.'

Gleeson has three thriving businesses, all to do with the liquor trade, and he believes that all three would suffer under a Labour government. His empire stretches from Feilding, where he lives, to Wellington, 100 miles south and to Wanganui, 60 miles north. Its cornerstone is the Empire Tavern in Feilding, just off the main street of the bustling North Island town that Gleeson says is one of the most prosperous of its size in New Zealand. The Empire Tavern is a pub with a staff of thirteen and last year it had a turnover of £250 000 (NZ$400 000).

Also contributing handsome profits are a wholesale liquor store in Wanganui (£33 000 or NZ$56 000) and a motel cum liquor store in Stokes Valley, Wellington (£44 000 or NZ$76 000). He mentions the Stokes Valley property with a capitalist's pride. 'Our taxable profit there was NZ$76 000, which would be unbelievable to most people because it was our first year. The year before it had gone into receivership. With that profit we have just purchased another property in Wanganui, which we are going to develop further for our wholesale business.'

At the Empire Tavern Gleeson rules. He is there from eight in the morning until closing time on Mondays, Tuesdays, Thursdays and Fridays in the winter, devoting the other days to his rugger. As well as being the All Blacks coach he is a North Island selector and on the panel of three national selectors. Out of the rugby season he puts in even longer hours at work. He refuses to allow into his pub those of whom he, as a strict disciplinarian, does not approve. They have to slake their thirst elsewhere in town. But for his rugby Gleeson would surely have become involved in local politics. By now, in his early fifties, he could probably have served several terms as mayor had he had time.

But nowadays there is little time for anything other than work and rugby. As a player he used to turn out for Feilding and Manawatu province in the centre or on the wing. He stopped playing when he was 28.

His last game for Manawatu was against Otago. It was an 11–11 draw. Eight days later he began coaching Feilding and developing his belief in running rugby. 'The most satisfying thing I find about coaching is taking men who have not been together before and developing them in your style of play. I've had colts sides and I've been able to teach them my style. I also developed the Junior All Blacks when they went to Argentina with me in 1976.'

In Argentina his young players stormed across the Pampas very successfully, scoring over four times as many points

(321–72) and nine times as many tries (48–5) as the Argentinians.

'With the All Blacks against the Lions I had a bit of difficulty because I had inherited a side that had just come back from South Africa under another coach, John Stewart. I found at times, and particularly in the second Test, that one half of the team were doing one thing and one half another.'

Gleeson's unobtrusive coaching style mirrors his personality. He stands to one side at training sessions, rarely dominating, and when he has a point to make he unostentatiously calls his men around him. From time to time he might slap a fist into an open palm. He is a most undemonstrative man. 'My wife says to me, "I can never have an argument with you because you will never argue back." That's me. My way of coaching is a quiet manner, not domineering and dictating.

'I don't think a player listens to a guy who sounds off and clenches his fist and raises his voice. As a player I can recall experiencing that and it went straight over my head. And I thought, players don't tolerate that. We are all human beings and they are all intelligent people playing the game. I am sure they are not going to react to a bombastic tone and swearing and demands. What you have to do is to put across your coaching policy, your philosophy, quietly. You can get more out of a player by extracting something from him and communicating with him than by shouting at him.'

It is a fascinating contradiction that Jack Gleeson, a cautious and rather shy man, should coach such an expansive and extrovert style of rugby. He wants all fifteen men to participate and the game to be attractive and flowing. The theory that a coach's tactics reflect his personality – as you are, so you coach – does not apply to Gleeson.

Rugby is a running game he says, a game for fifteen men. He and fellow selectors J.J. Stewart and Eric Watson were agreed in the series against the Lions that this was the way to play.

'In 1956 when the Springboks were here it was ten-man, possibly nine-man rugby. We won the series, sure, but that didn't do rugby any good in New Zealand. The youth are fairly intelligent people and if they want to be involved in sport they want to take part.

'I was a back and no way do you want to train twice each week and if you are in your rep side then four nights each week and all you get to do is to throw the ball in at the line out. It drove youth away from our game.'

As All Blacks coach he believes deeply that it is his job to make sure the youth come back to the game. When he took the All Blacks on an internal tour of New Zealand in 1972, soon after their defeat by the British Lions, he encouraged them to move the ball. By doing so they overcame an exhausting schedule of nine matches in three weeks to win all their games and score 63 tries.

Tragically, New Zealand's rugby administrators were not, at that time, prepared for such a drastic change from the basic style of solid forward play. Because they considered Gleeson's style of play too loose, he was overlooked as coach for the All Blacks tour of Britain and France in 1972/3. He wasn't hurt to be passed over, he says now. He felt honoured to be even a selector.

Instead Bob Duff was chosen and subsequently fired. He was succeeded by the popular J.J. Stewart but when the All Blacks lost the 1976 Test series in South Africa, it was Stewart's head that rolled as coach. He remained as a selector. So Gleeson's apprenticeship was long, before he received the nod for the series against the Lions in 1977 and the subsequent short tour to France.

But after the Lions series he ended up wearing the victor's laurel wreath. He had become the first New Zealand coach to win a major Test series in nearly ten years. The All Blacks had outscored the Lions by 6 tries to 3, in the main by playing fast open football. They had stayed true to their coach's rugby beliefs.

During the series Gleeson did not get on with John Dawes, the Lions coach. They were two very different men. Gleeson, 50, had never been an outstanding player. John Dawes, at 37, had already had a brilliant rugby career. Captain of Wales when they won a Grand Slam, captain of the conquering 1971 Lions in New Zealand, he retired and turned to coaching Wales with great success. He took over the assignment of coaching the 1977 Lions with the confidence and self-assurance that this record had bred.

Gleeson recalls their first meeting, at Masterton, and being so overwhelmed by Dawes's arrogance or self-assurance that he couldn't find anything to talk about. As the tour went on the gap between them widened.

Gleeson spoke out about what he called cheating by the Lions forwards at the game's trouble spot, the line out. He claimed that some of the Lions were jumping across the line and using their free hand to lever themselves up off their rivals' shoulders. 'If the Lions carry on they are going to cop trouble,' he warned.

Because Gleeson was who he was, his comments attracted a lot of attention. At the time John Dawes felt hurt and angry at Gleeson. The Lions had come to New Zealand knowing they would probably have to change their line-out jumping to cope with what in Britain would be considered illegal tactics. Even so Dawes claimed that his men still preferred the straight jump, the two-handed catch. 'Before we came out here we practised the two-handed catch. We wanted to do it but if we aren't allowed to then we must do the same as the New Zealanders.'

Later in the tour Gleeson criticized the Lions' backs for standing up offside. He said this was killing the attacking play of the All Blacks three quarters. 'If John is coaching that way and deliberately getting his backs into that position, he must also be getting his forwards to do illegal things. If that is what is happening that is why we are having so many problems. A coach who coaches like that is not developing rugby and back play at all. He is killing the game. He is better off out of rugby.'

'That is unbelievable,' snapped Dawes, when told of Gleeson's comments. 'A back is either on side or off side. It is there in the law book. It is either right or wrong. If I took Jack Gleeson seriously . . . well I would just laugh.'

So it went on, charge and counter charge until the two of them called an uneasy truce at the end of the tour.

In another respect Gleeson differed from Dawes. Gleeson is no lover of the fourth estate but he understands the need for journalists to be around. He does not have the *savoir faire* of, say, J.J. Stewart, his predecessor, and consequently there are many moral and other issues he will not discuss. The most obvious is South Africa. 'It is an issue that is far beyond me,' he has said. 'Who can cure it? Can you?'

He appreciates though, that it is part of a coach's job to help journalists. 'They are there, like that piece of furniture, that wall, that door. You can't do without them. You have got to get on with them.'

It was one of John Dawes's biggest failings in New Zealand in 1977 that he misunderstood and antagonized some journalists covering the tour. He resented being criticized and he resented British journalists criticizing British players. On occasions he even tried to keep the journalists away from the team.

From the sidelines Gleeson watched the running battles and was present at one of the last. At a party on the night of the fourth and final Test Dawes instructed that some journalists be thrown out even though some of them were present as guests of the players. 'Perhaps John hasn't lost enough,' Gleeson observed one day. 'I think it is an important part of being a coach – learning to lose. It has happened to all of us in our time.'

Gleeson believes in the purity of rugby, its ethos. He believes that today's players have a duty to demonstrate it as a clean, attractive game to the players of tomorrow. So when he says that it was not his doing that the All Blacks tactics in the second Test were, as one player admitted, 'to get anything in red' then one must accept his word for it. Most likely such tactics were laid in the ten or so minutes after Gleeson had left the dressing room before the team ran out onto Lancaster Park.

It is to his credit that he, among others, went 'crook' at Kevin Eveleigh in the dressing room after the game. Eveleigh had seemed most at fault as the All Blacks weighed into the Lions with late tackles and punches, and prompted some sordid off-the-ball play by both sides.

It is also to his credit that he had the courage to drop Eveleigh, a player from Feilding, Gleeson's own club. For that matter, the New Zealand selectors did the game a service by their handling of the young Manawatu scrum half Mark Donaldson who kicked Willie Duggan so blatantly during a game against the Lions that New Zealanders were horrified. For what were widely taken as disciplinary reasons, the very promising player was not considered for either of the first two Test matches.

So if one grants Gleeson his sincerity, and one must, so one must understand his sincerity when he adopts a prim, reactionary role about the vices of modern society. Argentina was a cathartic experience for him. He relished much of what he saw around him.

'After coming home from South America I was ashamed of our youth here in New Zealand, though any youth that takes part in sport – there is nothing wrong with them. Those watching and not playing it, I mean. The Argentinian beer is one-quarter as strong as ours and three times as expensive. So there is no drunkenness.' Such a puritanical view is surprising from one in the booze business.

'In the United States you never see any litter because they can be fined up to $200. I could take you out of here, out of my office, walk up the street and ask someone to pick up the litter. You know what they would tell you to do. Our blokes have too much money, too much grog and they get it too cheaply.'

Gleeson feels that South American values and their discipline in Argentina are more to his liking. 'You never see any vandalism,' he continued, 'and, as a player said, it is because the last guy who committed any vandalism is dead. To my mind that means discipline.'

Chapter 14

Second Test – Lions 13 All Blacks 9

The second Test, held at Lancaster Park Oval, Christchurch, will be remembered as Terry Cobner's Test. His mark was on the Lions team as clearly as a footprint left in wet sand. He was not officially a selector but as pack leader he chose the forwards he wanted and he laid down the tactics. He organized a forty-minute line-out practice for the forwards the day before the Test and then he quietly took aside Gordon Brown and Billy Beaumont, who were to play in the second row, and the No. 8, Willie Duggan, and told them: 'If we win this game it will be because of the ball you win in the line out. If we lose it, you will be blamed.'

Before the Lions took the field Cobner called his seven other forwards together. They moved across the changing room, the studs of their boots ringing out on the stone floor, and went into the lavatory, shutting the door behind them. Cobner wanted them completely on their own. He is an excellent motivator. His vocabulary is limited. He talks a language in keeping with the cold, bare stone floors of most rugby changing rooms. In these last minutes he appealed to their emotions. He pleaded with them and he said that he wanted his wife to be able to walk down the street in Pontypool with her head held high.

There was an air of determination about the Lions in those last hours. They had to win the Test to keep the series alive and it was their bad luck that they had to do it on a ground where no British Lions teams had ever before won a Test. Furthermore, no Lions side had ever won the second Test in New Zealand.

For the first time on tour all thirty Lions had been available for selection. Not one was injured. The selectors made six changes, five of them in the forwards, the department where the Lions were so badly beaten at Wellington the previous month.

The biggest surprise was that they had chosen Billy Beaumont, who was considered no better than the sixth best second row forward in Britain at the time the Lions party was announced in March. Clearly Cobner must have been impressed with the big Lancastrian, who had arrived in New Zealand only three and a half weeks earlier and had played only three games. 'Billy tightened things up for us enormously at the front of the line out,' said Cobner as early as the night of Beaumont's first game. 'He gets the ball from the kick-off, too.'

The other changes among the forwards were less surprising. Fran Cotton had rediscovered his form and was preferred at loose head to Phil Orr who had been uncomfortable against Kent Lambert at Wellington. The jut-jawed Cotton had the extra advantage over Orr of being able to win more ball at the front of the line out. The Englishman Peter Wheeler took over as hooker from Bobby Windsor, ending Windsor's run of five successive Test appearances. And in the second row Gordon Brown, having partially recovered from his shoulder injury, came in for Allan Martin.

'We got stuffed in the line outs in the first Test,' said Cobner, 'because we had nobody to support Willie Duggan. I can't jump against Kirky and neither can Trevor. You've got to have two No. 8s.' So the combative Derek Quinnell came back into the Test side and Swansea's Trevor Evans was dropped. The new-look pack of forwards was impressive. It had height, weight, physical presence and mobility.

The only change in the backs was a surprising one. Peter Squires, whom many considered to be a natural ball player even if he did lack pace, was dropped. J.J. Williams was moved to the right from the left where he had played in the first Test and the young Welshman, Gareth Evans made his Test début on the left wing.

The All Blacks meanwhile had their problems. The cornerstone of their scrum, Kent Lambert, their tight head prop, dropped out with appendicitis. On Thursday 7 July after failing a fitness test during All Blacks training at Lincoln College, twelve miles outside Christchurch, Grant Batty, their fiery left wing announced he was retiring from international rugby. His career as an All Black had spanned five years. His injured right knee, which had restricted him to only eleven first-class games since the end of 1975, forced Batty's decision. 'I would probably have retired when the season ended anyway,' said the impish little man, who was still only 25. 'I must admit that once I was in the first Test I thought I'd be there for the series. But the action of my knee is such that I can't compete at that level again.'

No sooner was this announcement made than All Blacks' coach Jack Gleeson declared Bruce Robertson, the talented centre from Counties, was unfit for the Test after being concussed in a game earlier in the week. Mark Taylor, who went to Argentina with the Junior All Blacks, replaced Batty and Otago's Lyn Jaffray came in for Robertson.

Back in the centre of Christchurch, latecomers prowled the streets seeking tickets for the Test. At Lancaster Park a helicopter was whipping up a draught as it hovered over the pitch to try and dry the pitch. The previous week a minor game attracting only 700 spectators had been played on it and it was badly cut up even before heavy rain fell on it. By the afternoon of the Test what had been a morass a week before had dried out sufficiently to leave two-thirds of the pitch looking reasonable. The middle third was a disgrace, however.

As it happened it didn't matter because the Test match will be remembered for things other than the muddy ground. It was in this game that the Lions forwards gave the first real indication they were becoming an exceptional force. The entire team showed courage, guts and character. The Lions might easily have been overawed by the occasion. Their need to win might have made them too defensive and edgy. Instead they attacked the All Blacks from the start and then held out against a mighty onslaught in the last twenty minutes. Their character was revealed by the way they dealt with the premeditated physical attack the All Blacks made on them, particularly on Bennett.

Early on in the game the Lions captain slipped on the wet turf and was badly done over by the All Black forwards. He rose to his feet, his mouth cut and bleeding, his confidence shaken. Later he was caught again by the opposition and he was being punched long after the ball had gone.

Worst of all, soon after half-time Bennett fielded a kick behind his own goal line and had kicked the ball into touch when flanker Kevin Eveleigh flew at him in an atrociously late tackle. Bennett went down, the Lions rushed back to help their precious team-mate – 'I always move a bit faster when I see that it is Benny who has been hurt,' says Gordon Brown – and fighting broke out. It wasn't the first time. Earlier Graham Price and Brad Johnstone detached from a line out; one punched, the other butted. As Price fell to the ground burly Billy Bush rushed up and kicked the helpless Lion more than once.

These incidents reminded observers of the tempestuous series between the Lions and the South Africans three years earlier. The All Blacks undoubtedly started the dirty play. One admitted afterwards 'we were out to get anything in red', but the Lions were not slow to retaliate. I saw a boot going at an All Black forward. Bryan Williams was late tackled. Some time after the game Jack Gleeson pointed out that his men had complained about the Lions too. 'They are pretty good at putting the boot in and running,' said Gleeson. 'Ian Kirkpatrick is very bitter towards Graham Price who kicked him, and Sid Going saw Terry Cobner hit Brad Johnston.'

The New Zealanders were probably frustrated at their lack of possession, their inability to get into the game. For the opening twenty minutes the Lions had complete control and in this time they made sure of victory.

Gareth Evans went close to scoring a remarkable try after he had hacked the ball thirty yards. Only the spin of the ball into touch at the last minute saved the All Blacks, for the full back Colin Farrell was caught out of position. Phil Bennett kicked a penalty when Sid Going was offside at a scrum. Then, after a period of testing Farrell with high kicks, the Lions scored their try, the only one of the game.

From a line out in mid-field Bennett chipped the ball cleverly through the advancing All Blacks. He darted past them quickly as they struggled to stop and turn on the slippery surface, and he kicked the ball on. Colin Farrell raced forward from full back but the ball rebounded to Bennett off Farrell's foot to be picked up by a Lion. Gordon Brown charged on with it; Derek Quinnell picked it up when the big Scotsman was stopped and he passed to Ian McGeechan.

The centre had J.J. Williams roaring alongside him and Andy Irvine who had raced up from full back was just behind and outside the wing. Racing across to cover were Sid Going, Farrell, who had by now regained his footing, and left wing Mark Taylor. 'As I made ground I heard Andy Irvine outside me calling for the ball,' said Williams as he relived the try later that night. 'But as I was about to pass to him I saw that he was covered.

'I delayed the pass momentarily, sold a dummy and cut back slightly inside to go over the line and score myself.' It was Williams's ninth try of the tour and Bennett's conversion attempt hit the right upright.

As if this was not enough of a helter-skelter start for the visitors, more was to come and the Lions threatened to run riot. Peter Wheeler, after taking a pass from Steve Fenwick ten yards from the All Blacks' line, was high tackled as he seemed certain to score a try on his Test début. The penalty was a formality for Bennett, taking the score to 10–0.

What would have happened then had Wheeler scored and Bennett converted the try? 6 points instead of 3 would have made it 13–0 to the Lions and the match would have been completely safe.

As it was the game swung slowly away from the Lions and towards the All Blacks. The massive forward dominance that was so noticeable in the opening twenty minutes had tired the Lions and, as if they were constantly being taunted, the All Blacks came back into the game, moving the ball at every opportunity.

The last twenty minutes were as hectic as the first had been. The Lions were lucky once when Bryan Williams missed a penalty from in front of the posts, a penalty that would have taken the score from 6–13 to 9–13 with ten minutes left. 'I was very worried at this stage,' Cob said later. 'I thought: oh Christ, we are going to let it slip. We had put in so much good work earlier on yet it was slipping away from us and everyone was aware of it.'

Time and again in this period the Lions had to defend desperately. Once it seemed all was lost when Colin Farrell penetrated their defence only for Phil Bennett to knock him over with the sort of tackle that makes a mockery of those oft-heard accusations that he shirks the physical. From the ruck the All Blacks switched the attack and, just as the alarm bells were sounding again for the Lions, Lyn Jaffray knocked on in midfield.

Still the All Blacks pressed. They mounted a siege and forced a line out almost on the Lions' line. A maul developed and Ian Kirkpatrick thrust his way past some red shirts before being held up. A scrum was ordered five yards from the Lions' line. This was Sid Going country, the place where he was most likely to make a burst on his own and rely on his strength and the support of his forwards to get over.

But as the All Blacks heeled the Lions drove forward and Quinnell and Cobner detached from the scrum. Going looked, saw his way was blocked by two wise Welshmen, and passed. Lyn Jaffray, who had just knocked on in midfield, was set up to take the ball on the burst. He caught it five yards from the Lions line right under the posts and, as every New Zealander in the stadium rose to acclaim the impending try, fumbled it and knocked on. Gareth Evans who had been drawn in from the left wing, swooped to touch down the loose ball. The score was 13–9 to the Lions.

In their changing room immediately after the game there were scenes of jubilation. Players wandered around in a daze. Cobner, naked save for a towel around his waist, sat staring at the floor. Periodically he raised his right hand in a gesture of silent superiority. He was near to tears. Probably the people in Pontypool were, too. They had been sitting up listening to their radios in the small hours of the morning and were undoubtedly very proud of 'their son'. Terry Cobner has a natural pride in his family, his home village of Abersychan, his rugby club Pontypool and his country. He is so strongly Welsh that he has named his daughters Rhiannon, Sian and Bethan 'so it's quite clear where they come from'. One of the proudest of all was surely Ray Prosser, the Pontypool club coach. Cobner and the jovial Pickwickian Prosser are as close as father and son and before the tour began the older man had told his young friend what to expect in New Zealand, based on his own experiences there with the Lions in 1959.

Nothing, however, could have prepared Cobner nor the rest of the Lions for the level of the hostility that was directed at them generally throughout their tour and particularly in this match. It was common for the Lions to be booed and whistled during their attempted penalty kicks and conversions. Few crowds and certainly not the one at Christchurch were prepared to acknowledge their good play.

How does one explain the barracking and hostility? At Christchurch spectators continually shouted, 'Hollywood' when a Lion was injured, even when it was clear that the player was not faking. As the final whistle blew in the Test match Brynmor Williams threw his arms in the air to celebrate. As he did so a spectator rushed into the pitch and punched him on the jaw.

A sound effects microphone had to be removed from the crowd because of the abusive language which, incidentally, was directed as much at the All Blacks as at the Lions. In Taumarunui, scrum half Douglas Morgan took a late tackle. As he was helped from the pitch with what was later described as a sprung rib cartilage, a spectator shouted out, 'Morgan is a wanker.'

After the Test the Lions were bitter. Three of the forwards said it was the dirtiest game they had ever played in. The All Blacks selectors seemed disappointed too. J.J. Stewart remarked, 'I would have much preferred the New Zealand Army Band to have played on for another hour and a half.' It was a sad end to a sad day for rugby. The Lions celebrated quietly that night.

Chapter 15

Mister Muldoon:
he also knows his rugby

'New Zealand is an isolated country, set in the middle of the Pacific Ocean.' I quote from a pamphlet published by the New Zealand migration office in London. It also says that the country has a population of three million and the average age of New Zealanders is 25. I had picked up the pamphlet when I went to New Zealand House to try and find out a little more about the country at the other end of the world I was about to visit.

From my schooldays I had only a slight knowledge of New Zealand. I knew that Wellington was the capital and I remembered a geography master explaining that Cook Strait was a turbulent stretch of water between the North and South Islands. I knew that Robert Muldoon was Prime Minister but I wasn't sure of his politics. I felt slightly ashamed to realize that I knew more about New Zealand's sporting history than any other aspect of the country.

I remembered the two famous Olympians, Peter Snell and the lonely figure of Murray Halberg. I had watched the 1967 All Blacks and at the Montreal Olympics I admired the courageous men's hockey team.

Trying to fill in the many gaps in my knowledge I came across an article in *The Guardian* newspaper. 'New Zealand is a film composed of a dream of a half-forgotten provincial England of the 1950s, a dream of missionaries, and a dream of a long-gone British Empire,' wrote Terry Coleman.

'Englishness is everywhere,' he wrote. 'Most of the cars are British but five, ten, twenty, some even thirty years old and still in general use. I saw a Jowett Javelin. There are thousands of small shops and most of the signs are unpainted. There are trolley buses. Most towns have silver bands. The domestic architecture is seaside British though in wood not brick.'

Looking back on three and a half months in the country, I don't think I could have put it better. Terry Coleman did not much like New Zealand. He complained about poor food, especially lamb, and he was right. Whatever dish one asked for it came on a plate creaking with mashed potatoes, chips and perhaps roast potatoes as well. 'Veges' were inclusive whether you liked it or not.

But I liked the country. I felt at home in the Hawke's Bay club in Napier with its wooden-panelled walls, its gracious curving staircase and roaring coal fire. The paper in Hawke's Bay is called the *Daily Telegraph*. On a Saturday morning Napier hummed and bustled just like many a genteel seaside town in England. I think back with affection to the Poverty Bay club in Gisborne, the four massive snooker tables in the games room, and next door one of the oldest squash courts in the country. These clubs were as British as the Reform Club in Pall Mall.

I was struck by the enormity of the country. Going to visit All Black Brian Lochore, I asked him the way from Masterton.

'Come straight out of town and we are the second turning on the right.'

'How far before we turn right?' I asked.

'About twenty miles,' he replied. 'But don't worry – there is only one turning. You can't miss it.'

Throughout New Zealand people were warm and open and the men in particular had a very colourful way of talking. I once overheard a New Zealander admiring a friend's beautiful car.

'Jeez, it's not a bad bus,' he said enviously.

'Aw, shit, it purrs along you know,' replied his friend.

The sheer sense of space in New Zealand was breathtaking. It was not at all unusual to be able to look for miles over rolling fields or rugged mountains and not to see a house or another person. I felt happiest in the Mediterranean climate at the top of the North Island where one could swim, sail and go hang-gliding nearly all the year round.

In New Zealand you were thousands of miles away yet so close to home. Streets in Christchurch in the South Island are named after English cathedral towns – Hereford, Worcester and Gloucester. The *New Zealand Herald*, the country's leading daily paper, still carries photographs of newly married couples with quaint accounts of the wedding: 'The matron of honour, Mrs Sue Evans, wore a classically styled turquoise crêpe gown under an overblouse of floral organdie in matching tonings. She carried a single rose.' On the *Herald*'s sports pages often appear announcements to the effect that, 'Mrs So and So holed in one at the Such and Such golf course yesterday.' Such stories often end, in breathless tones, 'Mrs So and So used a seven iron.'

New Zealanders are apparently, among the most inveterate travellers in the world, despite swingeing taxes on the already high air fares. Yet I often found I had been to places that New Zealanders, particularly those from the North Island, had never visited. They had holidayed in Fiji, climbed Table Mountain, seen the Crown Jewels in London. But they had never visited Westport or Timaru or Blenheim or New Plymouth.

It seemed to me as I looked back on my time in New Zealand that the country was desperately trying to jump from the 1950s straight into the 1970s. There were more and newer cars beginning to replace the bicycles and patched up old bangers that had done service for so long and still are doing so in so many cases. New Zealanders are a nation of sheep farmers – there are more sheep than people in the country – and now there is more money with which to buy mechanical aids for the farm. You could see the changes all round.

As their life changes so does their rugby. In New Zealand rugby is as important as it is in Llanelli, South Wales for example. But prior to the series against the Lions the All Blacks had gone for too long without winning a major Test series. They had never known a decade like it. They lost to South Africa in 1970 and again in 1976 and to the British Isles in 1971. The moans about the state of their beloved game by New Zealanders that greeted the Lions in May 1977 were long and genuine.

Coinciding with the start of the decline in popularity and success of rugby in New Zealand was the introduction of competitive soccer. First it was a league for ten teams. In 1976 two more teams were added. Each week British soccer games are shown on television and the big news the week the Lions arrived (to a much smaller welcoming crowd than had met the 1971 party) was of the Football Association's Cup Final to be played

12 000 miles away at Wembley between Manchester United and Liverpool. A live telecast was shown in New Zealand in the middle of the night and viewing figures indicated an enormous interest.

Perhaps, then, it was a combination of an excessive desire to see their men win and a decline in standards noticeable throughout the world that made the crowds at Wellington for the first Test, at Canterbury for the second, at Whangarei for the north Auckland game, so overtly hostile to their visitors from Britain. There was something rotten in the state of rugby all right, but why?

In Wellington one day, Prime Minister Muldoon gave me an interview. I asked him why he thought it was. 'My feeling is that it has very largely been a product of the style of rugby in particular games,' Mr Muldoon replied. 'I have seen three Tests on television and I have followed and watched rugby all my life. The hostility of the crowd is directly related to brutality on the field. I think it is no more than that.

'You have a very vigorous pack of forwards,' Mr Muldoon continued. 'You will recall the occasion when that young flanker was knocked cold and had to leave Athletic Park.' He was referring to the game between the Lions and New Zealand Juniors when Jon Sullivan was knocked unconscious in a tackle by Lions forward Fran Cotton. 'The reaction lasted for some time in that game,' said Muldoon. 'Long after the incident had passed by. You will find the same in provincial rugby in New Zealand.'

I suggested that the hostility might have something to do with the pommy-bashing campaign tactics Mr Muldoon's National Party adopted during the general election in 1975. As he toured the country seeking votes, Muldoon was fond of referring, with scorn in his voice, to British trade union migrants bringing in suicidal class warfare to New Zealand. He talked specifically of a 'Clydeside mentality'.

'Surely it is possible to be selective in criticizing migrants,' said Mr Muldoon. 'I was referring to trade unionists and not the British in general. I know of many British people who tell me they came to New Zealand to get away from that sort of thing and I applaud that. Some of the leaders of our most militant unions come from a very tough trade unions atmosphere in

Leo the mascot was stolen late in the tour but doubtless not by this happy rooster.

Willie Duggan is the one on the right. His friend is an inscrutable Maori carving in Rotorua.

Price, Wheeler, Cotton, the three wise men. Labouring at the pit face, they were magnificent.

Broon of Troon felt safer on the whole with two feet on the ground. Luckily, there is someone driving.

Only a cannon could split the second row and golfing partners Beaumont and Brown.

Elgan — the boys called him Harry — Rees enjoyed ice cream and chocolate sauce more than pool or snooker.

Derek Quinnell would rather have played more rugby and less pool. But injuries and bad weather gave him no choice.

Wife Janet promises to hold Peter Squires to the message on his apron. Bruce Hay attacks the other end.

Twice a week Cobner received letters from home. Desperately homesick, he could have done with them twice a day.

Even in the tensest moments Steve Fenwick could produce the appropriate quip. Benny laughs at the latest just before boarding a plane.

Britain. They have brought a class-warfare attitude into trade
unions which we deplore and which I thought we had just about
got rid of.'

There was one particularly aggravating feature I found living
in hotels and motels in New Zealand, which I put down to union
zeal. If one arrived so much as a minute late for a meal then one
was not served. There was not room for compromise or negotia-
tion. 'The chef's shut down and gone home,' I was told at a
motel in Masterton when I arrived no more than one minute late
for breakfast.

New Zealanders were divided about Mr Muldoon. They
either loved him or hated him, and in rugby clubs I found many
more who loved than hated him, because he tried to keep politics
out of sport.

He does not have much time for journalists. Trendy lefties,
demented hens and nit-pickers he has called them in recent
times.

Mr Muldoon, a conservative in every way, dresses soberly.
The day of my interview he wore a dark suit, white shirt,
regimental tie and black shoes.

He was curt and far from warm or welcoming. An obsequious
male secretary ushered us in to the Prime Minister's office on
the third floor of the new Parliamentary building in Wellington,
named the Beehive because of its shape. Muldoon stood looking
at some papers for a moment and then hurried over to sit in an
armchair under a window. He made no gesture of welcome or to
shake hands. In fact the impression he gave was one of impa-
tience as he plumped up the cushions and demanded to know
how long we wanted.

'Half an hour,' I said.

He shook his head. 'Fifteen minutes. I have to speak in the
House at quarter to five. You can have until then.'

I made the point to the Prime Minister that I had just spent
nearly three months travelling throughout New Zealand. I had
spoken informally in bars, formally at rugby clubs and everywhere, from Invercargill to Pukekohe, it was obvious to me that
the average New Zealander was bitter about the way his country
was treated at the 1976 Olympics.

Was New Zealand picked out to be used as a political football
because she was small, easy to bully and politically unimportant

I asked? Cr was it perhaps because Mr Muldoon and his colleagues had made it a part of their election campaign in 1975 that they would welcome sporting contacts with South Africa were they to be elected?

Muldoon had a ready answer, as he shook his head to indicate that it was neither. 'There were two reasons,' he said. 'First, rugby is the national game in both New Zealand and South Africa and so it assumes an importance in these things over and above, say a team of trampoline experts from the United States going to South Africa or vice versa.' He paused here and gave a slow smile at his joke.

'Secondly we had two very active organizations – CARE (Citizens Association for Racial Equality) and HART (Halt All Racist Tours) – and they sent overseas a stream of material to African governments in particular. Most of it was incorrect.' He suggested, as an example of an inaccuracy, that the All Blacks had been paid to go to South Africa to play rugby against the Springboks in 1976. 'That is a lot of nonsense. You cannot pay a rugby team. They would be debarred from playing rugby if they took payment. But the story went around the world.'

The other thing that was puzzling New Zealanders, I told the Prime Minister, was his Government's stance over South Africa. Remembering the National Party's declarations of love and support for South Africa, New Zealanders now found it hard to follow Mr Muldoon's new line of thought – dictated by the Gleneagles agreement – an agreement aimed at vigorously combating 'the evil of apartheid'.

He ducked the issue slightly. 'The Gleneagles agreement says "drawing a curtain across the past". In other words forget everything up to now, and then it ends up by saying hopefully we will all go to Edmonton to watch the Commonwealth Games.'

'Wasn't this an about-face?' I asked.

'I don't think so,' he replied curtly.

'Well then, what is the position about sporting contacts with South Africa?'

'I have said that there will be no significant exchanges with South Africa until such time as South African sport is truly integrated,' said Muldoon, glancing at the clock and stroking his tie with his left hand. 'I don't think we are going to see another

South African rugby team in New Zealand until they've got thoroughly integrated rugby.'

Yet the Prime Minister could not confirm categorically that there would be a ban on such visits. The present New Zealand government did not want sports teams to go to South Africa nor teams from South Africa to visit New Zealand. That was all he would agree on.

'But if a team were to go against your wishes would there be anything you could do to stop them?' I asked. He agreed there was nothing that could be done and added, 'That is precisely the same as in Britain and I think as in Canada.'

'Perhaps you would issue a public statement deploring it?' I suggested.

He hedged. 'We would do what we have done with respect to the five rugby players who have decided to go to South Africa for the Celebration rugby games, and say that we are very disappointed but that it is their decision. We have made it quite clear that the final decision whether or not to go to South Africa rests with the sporting bodies.'

He stood up. 'I'm afraid I must go,' he said curtly. He strode over to his desk, picked up some papers and left through a side door. As he went out he shouted over his shoulder, 'You can find your own way out I expect.'

He struck me as a slightly sad figure, small, with a malformation in his left cheek that exaggerated any movement of his mouth and distorted smiles. His nickname was Piggy. At times in our chat he had been helpful and informative; at other times, prickly and brusque. 'I think that if you play back your tape you will find I have already answered that question,' he snapped at one stage. He was like a man always on the defensive, used to being under attack. And that, I supposed as I left his office, was precisely what he was. Come to think of it, that was what New Zealand was in sport – a nation under attack.

Chapter 16

Lousy lovers

At breakfast-time on Friday 22 July, I picked up the telephone and dialled John Dawes's room two floors above in the Royal International Hotel, Auckland. I wanted to talk about the tour and to know how the players felt. The tour had entered a difficult stage now. There were numerous injuries. It continued to rain and pitches were often covered with mud. Players were homesick and withdrawn, and hostile New Zealand newspaper attacks on them were just beginning. And there were only eight days left before the third Test.

The difficulties had all happened at once. After trailing 4–7 at half time, the Lions had just edged home 18–13 against Waikato, supposedly a second-division side. In the midweek game against the New Zealand Juniors the Lions had wallowed in mud so thick that they soon became indistinguishable even to one another. They knew a team-mate from an opponent only by the sound of the voice.

What had once been irritations, perhaps even things to laugh about, were now serious. Terry Cobner, a nervous traveller anyway, had been very frightened by a bad flight from Hamilton to Wellington when the pilot, unannounced, pitched the plane into a steep turn immediately after take off. Unaware of what was happening when the plane began to bank, Cobner looked at Ian McGeechan on his left for reassurance. McGeechan was the most knowledgeable Lion about flying and if he was happy then the worried ones knew they had nothing to worry about either. 'I said to him, "What's up Geech?" ' Cobner said later. 'He said, "I don't know." He was holding on to his seat with both hands and his knuckles were white. He looked really scared and that made me feel very frightened. I got up into the aisle and I wanted to run somewhere. I don't know where I thought I'd go I'm sure, but I just wanted to get off the plane. It was the worst feeling I have ever had.'

After arriving in Wellington Cobner discovered that the leg injury he had received against Waikato had turned septic. He was admitted to hospital in Wellington to have it drained, and became so depressed and homesick that he said he wanted to go home. Other injured Lions at this time included Derek Quinnell, who twisted an ankle in training in Wellington, Brynmor Williams, the first choice Test scrum half who was only slowly recovering from a hamstring injury, and winger Peter Squires, also bothered by a hamstring. Poor Cobner was left behind in the Lower Hutt hospital in Wellington as the rest of the team travelled on to Auckland.

So the morning I saw Dawes he was worried about his men. 'Are the lads enjoying it?' he wondered as he sat up in bed. 'On the way to a match we normally sing on the bus, albeit rather feebly. But on Wednesday, against the Juniors, there was nothing. They were dead tired. Yesterday at training I gave them touch rugby and soccer and that was it. I could sense that they wouldn't take anything else. Cob is very down,' Dawes continued. 'The doctor says that his injury is quite serious but that normally he would recover quite quickly. If he were up to here,' and Dawes held his left hand up to his neck, 'he would recover quickly. The trouble is he is down here.' He lowered his hand to the edge of his bed. 'It could take time. He wanted to come to Waitangi with us next week but the doctor said no. The other thing is he won't fly if he can help it. I was with him all Sunday evening at the Wellington supporters' club party, and there were birds and booze all around. He must have drunk gallons of beer but I couldn't get him to relax. His knees were still knocking as we left to come back to the hotel.'

The tiredness had begun to set in after the Lions' victory in the second Test. They were so emotionally drained by that victory down in damp Dunedin that it was a good bet they would lose to the Maoris the following Wednesday. 'I said to Dod the night before the game, "We're in trouble. I just can't get the boys up for it."'

Against the Maoris the Lions chose ten of those who had not

played in the Test and then buttressed them with five from the Test-winning side – backs Fenwick and J.J. Williams, and forwards Duggan, Cobner, who was captain, and Cotton. The already long odds against a British win looked longer when Fenwick was replaced by Gibson when his groin injury did not clear up in time. Two hours before kick-off Cobner withdrew with a hamstring. Trevor Evans took his place and also took over the captaincy.

Some flamboyant attacking play by the Maoris gave them a lead of 13–3 at half-time. Sid Going barrelled over for two tries and the Lions were reeling, punch drunk in the face of the onslaught launched by Tane Norton and his men. When Osborne dodged over for his side's third try, soon after half-time, to make the score 19–6, the Maoris were on the point of a famous victory.

It was not to be. The Lions brought off the greatest recovery of the tour. They scored two tries in three minutes starting with one from a penalty ploy. Players whizzed off in all directions and suddenly there was Tony Neary haring upfield. He sped fifty yards, passed to Gibson who then looped around Peter Squires and when the wing was stopped Gibson was able to score in the corner. Prop forward Phil Orr, stretching to make the line, got the next try. The score had narrowed to 19–14 now. Irishmen were everywhere. Two more tries in three minutes, both by Squires, locked the door on the bemused Maoris. It had been daylight robbery at Eden Park on a sunny afternoon and the 52 000 spectators buzzed with excitement as they left the ground.

Allan Martin was particularly pleased. The night before, while he was in the cinema watching *A Star is Born,* his wife gave birth to a little girl back in Wales. Martin's mother-in-law had called earlier in the evening to report that her daughter Janet had gone into hospital but it was Gordon Brown who actually told Martin the good news. Brown has a little daughter himself so he had a keen understanding of the Welshman's feelings at that time.

'I phoned the hospital immediately and spoke to the ward sister. She reassured me that everything was all right,' said Martin. 'I was so happy. I phoned my wife at six in the morning New Zealand time on Wednesday and the first thing she said to me was, "I'm OK and the baby is OK." Then she said, "Play well and get back into the Test side." Well, after that I just had to do something against the Maoris, didn't I?'

As Dawes watched his men fight back into a game that he thought was lost, he was a proud man. 'I regard the winning of that game as even greater than winning the second Test,' he said in our conversation that Friday morning. 'There you saw the true character of this team.' Character was something he mentioned often in our conversation. It was on his mind.

The reason was obvious. *New Zealand Truth,* a high-circulation weekly tabloid newspaper, had carried a story on the front page of the current issue saying the Lions were louts. With a banner headline above, the story began: 'The Lions make a great pack – of animals. The touring British Isles rugby side is a disgrace to its members and their homeland. There has been only one word to describe their behaviour since the team arrived here – DISGUSTING.'

The story went on to describe how during their stay at Wellington after the first Test two of the Lions urinated down a stairwell and some of their team-mates ripped seven hotel doors off their hinges. It claimed that in another town Lions threw glasses, turned over tables, uncoiled fire hoses and sprayed water.

On Friday morning Dawes was still burning with anger over this story. 'Normally if something like this appeared we would not take any notice of it at all because it is all lies. But the hostility over here to the boys is so great. I've never known anything like it.

'I read these things and I think of our lads. They're not angels, mind, but when I think back to the 1972/3 All Blacks and try to think of what has gone wrong I can't. They [the All Blacks] had some nasty players. We don't have any like that. I just can't work it out.'

Worse was to come though. The day after the third Test, the *Sunday News,* an Auckland tabloid newspaper with the biggest circulation in New Zealand, headlined their main story of the day on the front page: "THEY'RE LOUSY LOVERS." It was a story by a girl who claimed to have slept with four Lions. 'I found them boring, self-centred, ruthless, always on the make and anything but exciting bedmates,' she revealed. 'Give me the down-to-earth Kiwi male any day.'

The Lions were hurt and angry. Not only had their bedroom intimacies been splashed all over a newspaper but their masculinity was offended, too. Whether the 1977 Lions were better or worse than any other team, including the All Blacks, is unimportant. Such matters are normally part of the unwritten fabric of a rugby tour.

The damage that was done, the wrecking, was generally an expression by the Lions, often when they were drunk, of their disapproval of their accommodation. They found the Hotel St George in Wellington so unhelpful and inconsiderate that, fuelled by beer and disappointed after their loss in the first Test, they took childish revenge by smashing doors. They later paid NZ$500 for repairs.

One night two Lions hosed a woman out of bed in her hotel room in Christchurch. They apologized the next morning both to the woman concerned and the hotel manager and paid NZ$80 to repair the sodden carpets.

At Whangarei, where they played North Auckland, the Lions were put in rooms that were so small they could hardly hold a bed and a couple of suitcases. Even the most mild tourists thought the Wangarei Hotel was rather poor and, again in a drunken childish outburst, they did some wrecking.

If the Lions felt happy and well looked after they generally behaved themselves. The best example was at Pukekohe, near Auckland, where they found they had to share three to a room. This was irritating and they felt cramped, but the hotel staff more than compensated by their friendliness, serving meals at all hours and screening telephone calls. Not a speck of damage was done to this hotel.

During three very happy days and nights in Fiji, the total damage done to the team's hotel was the dumping of some steel-framed reclining chairs into the swimming pool. They were fished out the next morning undamaged.

The ethos of rugby encourages childish stupidity by grown ups, stupidity that is inexplicable in the cold light of day. So does too much drink, which seems as much a part of a rugby tour as boots and rugby balls.

One night I took three Lions out to dinner at a seafood restaurant in the Bay of Islands in the north of New Zealand's north island. The Scot Ian McGeechan, who lives in Leeds, and Welshmen Allan Martin and Trevor Evans were as representative of the Lions as any three players could have been. Originally from working-class backgrounds, they were much the same age: Martin 28, Evans 29 and McGeechan 30. Martin and McGeechan held the most common job among rugby players, that of school teachers, while Evans was a valuer and estate agent in Ammanford, Swansea. All three were married. McGeechan was the exception in not having any children and was also the only one of the three who had been a Lion before – South Africa, 1974.

They wore their blazers and flannels to come out to dinner. Over smoked marlin followed by enormous portions of hot scallops, snapper, whitebait, shrimps and raw oysters, washed down by red and white wine, we talked.

I said I thought that as a Welshman from an industrial part of South Wales Martin should be a socialist. 'Deep down I suppose I am,' he replied. 'But it seems to me that more and more of the socialist principles don't work these days. Nationalized industries don't work.'

McGeechan was the same, a socialist by nature but now tending towards the Tory party. 'I don't think enough money is being put back into circulation,' he said, sounding like a financial gnome from Zurich. 'It seems to be wrong these days to make a profit. There is far too much bureaucracy. And do you know,' he asked, looking serious for a moment and gesticulating to emphasize his point, 'there are seven non-productive workers in Britain for every productive worker?'

Just as Evans was about to explain his political beliefs, a waitress came to take our orders for dessert. On the table next to us a little boy played happily while his parents finished their meal. Seeing other little children we couldn't help but be reminded of own own. For a few moments we all indulged in our private memories.

Martin's brisk Welsh accent ended the nostalgia. 'What are boysenberries, Geech?' he asked as he studied the menu the waitress had just handed to him.

'A cross between a strawberry and a raspberry made by a man

named Boysen,' McGeechan replied quickly. Martin and Evans looked at their colleague with admiration.

'You're a fund of information, Geech,' Martin said. 'Most of it useless.'

We all ate boysenberries and cream and the proprietor joined us, bringing Irish coffees in half-pint mugs. A waitress came over with a menu for us to sign and on the top of it McGeechan wrote 'super meal' and added his signature before passing it around the table.

The proprietor's name was Trevor and he had left Cornwall, England, when he was three. He talked reverently about Sid Going, who had a farm just over the hill. He asked about Britain, which he had last visited twenty years earlier, and he listened while we described how the old country had changed. We talked together far into the night and when we went outside we could see the lights of Russell twinkling across the bay. Below where we had parked the car waves washed gently on the shore.

I drove the half-mile back to the hotel slowly and thoughtfully. They didn't seem like louts and animals to me. Maybe the New Zealand press stories were exaggerated but, in essence, they were true. Why it is that grown-up responsible men, teachers some of them, turn into wreckers, I just don't know.

Chapter 17

Third Test –
Lions 7 All Blacks 19

The third Test, down in Dunedin's Carisbrook Stadium in the South Island, should have been Phil Bennett's finest hour, the moment the popular little Welshman would captain the Lions to victory and a 2–1 lead in the four-game Test series. Everybody seemed to expect just that.

One week before the Test, the Lions had demolished the highly-fancied Auckland team 34–15, 5 tries to 1, a result that sent a scare round New Zealand. Later the Lions heard the announcement of the All Blacks team for the third Test with barely concealed delight. The three New Zealand selectors had panicked, the Lions thought, in making as many as six changes from the team defeated 13–9 in the second Test. The new team seemed to be weaker in some positions, and the sheer number of changes seemed to indicate a lack of confidence in the All Blacks' camp.

They had dropped prop forward Brad Johnstone, who won some useful line out ball, and brought in the burly Taranaki farmer, John McEldowney. Kevin Eveleigh was replaced as flanker by Graham Mourie, who had captained the Junior All Blacks in Argentina the previous summer. Brian Ford replaced Mark Taylor on the left wing, and at full back the selectors were risking a 21-year-old, Bevan Wilson. Having recovered from the concussion that kept him out of the second Test, Bruce Robertson regained his rightful place in the centre.

Yet what surprised the Lions most was that the great scrum half Sid Going was axed even from the replacements. He was a man they feared, and on this tour he had scored more tries against them – three – than any other New Zealander. Lyn

Davis, a 33-year-old tomato farmer, was chosen instead to serve alongside his Canterbury partner Doug Bruce.

After the Auckland game the Lions went up to the beautiful Bay of Islands and spent two days resting. All talk of rugby was banned as they swam in the heated pool, played golf on the beautiful rolling course outside their bedroom windows, and went deep-sea fishing. When their team for the Test was announced there was only one change from the team victorious at Christchurch – David Burcher in for Ian McGeechan in the centre. Incidentally, only two changes were made from the side that had played so impressively against Auckland. The Lions set off on their 800-mile journey down to Dunedin refreshed and confident.

As Carisbrook filled with the 40 000 spectators on the afternoon of the game, what was uppermost in the minds of the New Zealand rugby authorities was that there should not be a repeat of the brawling and booing that had marred the second Test three weeks earlier. The tannoy crackled into life and a metallic voice said: 'Ladies and Gentlemen, there is an estimated television audience of 22 million for this game. Let us show them what true New Zealand sportsmanship is.'

Incessant rain had become a part of the New Zealand scene and it fell again as All Black wing Bryan Williams kicked off and the Lions cleared his kick back into touch. At the line out McEldowney burst around the front, a ruck formed, and the ball came back sweetly and swiftly for the All Blacks. It went quickly from Lyn Davis to Bruce to Osborne to the elegant centre Bruce Robertson. Bryan Williams crashed infield to confuse the Lions but he did not touch the ball. As he did so Bevan Wilson raced up outside Robertson. The centre could have passed to Wilson. 'Some might say I should have done,' said Robertson, a tall, slim man with a fresh face and an easy smile. 'But when I looked at him I didn't think he could get in. So I kicked.' It was a beautiful kick that bounced to his left, away from Andy Irvine as the Scot ran across and away, too, from Phil Bennett as the Lions captain desperately tried to stop the attack. Ian Kirkpatrick swooped onto it as it bobbled over the Lions' line and touched it down for his fiftyeth try for New Zealand. Bevan Wilson converted. Less than one minute's play had elapsed and the score was 6–0.

Four minutes later Bennett put in a lovely rolling kick that dribbled into touch one yard from the All Blacks line. A maul followed the inconclusive line out and a scrum was ordered with the put-in given to the Lions as the team going forward. As the All Blacks wheeled the Lions scrum, Brynmor Williams picked up the ball and broke down the blind side. Bryan Williams stopped him but Willie Duggan, the Lions' No. 8, was close behind and he grabbed the ball and dived over the line to score. Bennett's conversion attempt from the touchline was hooked wide of the posts. With the score now only 6–4 to the All Blacks, the Lions' hopes began to rise once more.

The hectic pace continued and in the eleventh minute left wing Brian Ford dashed to within one yard of the Lions' line. He was stopped but cleverly made the ball available and a ruck formed. The big lock Andy Haden picked up the ball and charged, bull-like, at the line. He got over in the corner, much as Willie Duggan had moments earlier.

Bennett had a chance to reduce the All Blacks lead midway through the half. An All Black committed an offence at a line-out and Bennett's penalty kick was from 30 yards and slightly to the right of the posts. It was the difficult side of the field for him, a right footer using the instep kick, and he pulled it to his left, across the posts.

At half-time the All Blacks led 10–4. This was worrying for Bennett whose hopes of glory were beginning to fade. His kicking, apart from his line kicking, was poor. He had missed that one penalty, which he should have kicked. Furthermore, it was clear that Brynmor Williams at scrum half wasn't fully fit. Williams shouldn't really have played, for on the previous day he had not been well enough to take a full-scale fitness test on the injured hamstring in his left leg. With ten minutes of the first half remaining, J.J. Williams pulled a hamstring and had to be replaced by Ian McGeechan, which weakened the Lions as McGeechan was playing out of position.

The pitch was in surprisingly good condition considering it had rained for days. To protect it the Otago authorities had not allowed a game to be played at Carisbrook for the previous five weeks and the inevitable helicopter whirred over the ground for an hour on the morning of the match. It certainly wasn't so slippery that the advantage the Lions forwards had in scrummaging was nullified by them being unable to get proper purchase with their feet. At the very first scrum of the game the New Zealand forwards were rolled backwards by the Lions with a disdain that must have made Colin Meads sick as he sat in the stand. When was the last time New Zealand forwards were treated so disrespectfully?

But behind this magnificent platform, the Lions kicked away too much of the ball in attempting to unnerve Bevan Wilson at full back. They had failed to test Colin Farrell in the high wind at Wellington in the first Test when the blond Auckland full back was making his debut. They seemed to want to make sure that they didn't neglect to test Wilson. It didn't work and there were signs that the All Blacks three quarters were stronger than the Lions in quick passing and running.

Soon after the second half began Williams limped off and Doug Morgan replaced him. Then Bennett missed a penalty 20 yards out and slightly right of the posts. He hung his head in shame. As the half wound on his forwards continued to dominate. By the end they had won the line outs 24–14. The All Blacks front row had conceded two tight heads to the ever-alert Lions trio of Price, Wheeler and Cotton. But Bennett's play got worse and worse. He never was the straightest runner and now he was almost running sideways and then ballooning passes to his centre. Time and again the centre would receive both man and ball. Sometimes the Lions backs didn't even reach the gain line on their own ball.

Andy Irvine kicked a penalty from 30 yards that made the score 10–7, only for Bevan Wilson five minutes later to kick a similar length one and take the All Blacks to 13–7. For twenty minutes or so the Lions forwards dominated but another penalty by the inspired Wilson and an opportunist drop goal right on the whistle ended the scoring and left the All Blacks victors by the flattering margin of 19–7.

It was a sad and disappointed Lions team that left the ground. Just what had gone wrong, and how had Bennett's moment of glory been ruined? The answer was it was ruined largely by himself. If ever confirmation were needed that back play in Britain had not advanced in the previous few years then it was presented here.

What had happened was that the traditional roles of New

Zealand and British rugby had been reversed. The forward giants at Carisbrook were the men in red and the darting, elusive backs who could exist on less than an equal supply of ball were those of New Zealand. What irony that the transformation in the traditional roles of the teams should be on the very ground where eighteen years earlier in 1959 Lions had scored 4 tries to New Zealand's none. Yet the Lions lost that Test when Don Clark kicked 6 penalty goals to give his side a 1-point victory. A combination team of the Lions' forwards and New Zealand's backs would, on this form have been a brilliant team.

The reversal of roles may have been the main reason contributing to the victory of the New Zealanders but there were others.

Between them, Bennett and Irvine missed six out of seven attempts at goal, a failure rate more normally associated with New Zealand teams than the Lions, who in previous matches had managed almost a fifty per cent success rate. The question then was, should Bennett be dropped for the fourth Test? Had his nerve gone at the crucial moment? He looked a doleful figure as he walked around after the Test with a blackened eye, a slight cut on his nose, and his sad, rather forlorn air.

I had suggested before the tour began that I didn't think he was the man to lead the Lions, and I think the events in Carisbrook proved me right. Bennett's play overall in New Zealand had not been good by his own standards. His scrum halves were not able to give him either the length or speed of service he was used to from Gareth Edwards when playing for Wales or even Selwyn Williams at Llanelli. Yet Bennett, loyal to the death, wouldn't hear a word of criticism about them.

He was a good captain and very popular with his team-mates but the pressure of the captaincy had a bad effect on his game. And when his own play deteriorated then the cares of captaincy didn't help. His personality was more suited to being led than to leading. You don't burden a genius with mundane chores like making twenty-five aftermatch thank-you speeches, and appointing him the titular leader of men, some of whom were far stronger personalities and better suited to the captaincy than he.

His particularly bad performance in the third Test is not easily explained. Despite the holiday in Waitangi he was tired and depressed because he was never able to play at his best. He needs firm grounds on which to sidestep but the rain spoilt most of the pitches he played on.

'I played badly on the day and I knew it myself. Nobody had to tell me. But a lot of people came to me afterwards, people who had played rugby, and said "Christ, I had a lot of those when I played. Just get on and play the game." I was down, I played very badly that day and that was it. I think you are entitled to one bad game.'

Bennett also pointed out that the Lions tour of New Zealand was about three weeks longer than a Lions tour of South Africa. In South Africa the Lions played their last match eleven weeks and five days after leaving London airport. Eleven weeks and five days after leaving in 1977, the Lions woke up in Dunedin after losing the third Test the previous day. They still had another thirteen days before the final Test.

'I've felt homesick on this tour and I have had my down periods as every other player has,' says Bennett, 'but it hasn't been half as bad as it was in South Africa because I knew what to expect from this one.' He didn't send as many postcards from New Zealand as he had from South Africa – only 214.

'I usually write every other day and phone regularly. I love speaking to my son Steven. He is now 2 and I thought he would have forgotten me but apparently he can still pick me out of a team photo. I was being interviewed on television and he saw me. He tried to kiss the television and grab hold of it and when the interview finished and I went off the screen he cried for about half an hour. My wife couldn't stop him crying.'

Chapter 18

Bludgers

As the Lions tour wound on, an ever-increasing number of supporters followed them around New Zealand. Some wore jeans and anoraks, carried rucksacks and were hitch-hiking, sleeping where they could. Chirpy and boisterous, often with cans of beer in their hands, they were the nucleus of a group of supporters who were doing the tour on a shoestring. 'We're all rugby fanatics,' said Welshman Huw Prosser who had seen every game the Lions played. 'Well you have to be, don't you, to throw in your job and come 12 000 miles, don't you?'

Others travelled in comfortable coaches that swept them from their hotel to the ground and back again. They were mostly middle-aged prosperous businessmen, doctors, farmers, estate agents, some with their wives. One couple had even brought their children. The men wore blazers with badges marked British Lions Supporters' Tour 1977. Their three-week package trip was costing at least £1200 per person and probably nearer £1500. For Bill Bonus, a farmer from Cumbria, it was his first major trip, the first time he had ever been in an aeroplane. 'If you've never been more than a foot off the ground you get bloody scared. I had to have a few drinks before take-off but I'm OK now.'

Though they shared a love of rugby and were dominated by Welshmen there was one big difference between the two groups. 'They've got the money, we're the real boys,' said Prosser.

Rabid rugby enthusiasts whose sole aim was to watch the Lions, they were strangers to one another and made their separate ways to New Zealand. The first of the young bucca-neers to arrive was Nick Bird, an Englishman who had worked on a building site in London to raise the money for his trip. Bird, soon to be nicknamed Major after the character in Fawlty Towers, reached Auckland even before the Lions – on 1 May. One week later solicitor Mark Hancock flew in, after giving up his job in a practice in Swansea.

Early in June Welshman Kevin O'Brien left Cardiff docks where he was working and flew to Singapore. Then he took a boat to Perth in Western Australia and hitch-hiked eastwards to Sydney before picking up a plane to Auckland. Martin Hare, who came from Moseley near Birmingham, had worked in Australia for three months on his way out, as had Richard Davies, a soft-spoken Welshman. Hare arrived for the Lions' first game, Davies for their seventh.

There was one brave girl, Carol Dickson. She was a nurse from Edinburgh but like some of the others had been working in Australia for some time. Aged 23, she was one of the youngest, yet she had had months of experience hitch-hiking around Europe and South America.

These supporters had a refreshing enthusiasm. After a while they became like walk-on performers in a play, appearing and disappearing, not a central part of the action but a part that would have been missed had they not been there.

Many of them had been in New Zealand for some weeks but it was not until late June when the Lions played in Timaru in the South Island that they all got together. After that they began to meet on the halfway line after each game, travelled together where possible and swapped accommodation addresses. Their motto was, 'Eat when you can, sleep when you can, and wash when you can.'

As most of the money had gone on their air tickets to New Zealand, they were forced, after they arrived, to travel, eat and live as cheaply as possible. They had budgeted for £1000 (NZ$1700) spending money, but were treated to so much New Zealand hospitality that by the end of the tour they had not spent anything like as much. 'I've seen every game since the first Test and I have had to pay only for six nights' accommodation," said Richard Davies, two nights before the fourth and final Test. 'I have only had to pay for three nights in that time,' added Nick Bird.

The New Zealanders genuinely wanted to show off their

country, their homes, and their families, even to people they had never met before. 'The hospitality was fantastic,' said Carol. They had free meals, free accommodation and once when they were lost late at night even got a twenty-five-mile taxi ride in a police car.

'Four of us were walking past a railway station early one morning when some of the shunters stuck their heads out of their engines and called us,' remembers O'Brien. 'The major went to have a word with them, and the next minute we were having a cup of tea and were chatting away with them. They gave us their tea and sandwiches, which was very nice, and then took us for a hundred-mile ride at two o'clock in the morning just because we were Lions supporters.'

They developed a talent for what New Zealanders call bludging – surviving on their wits. They crossed Cook Strait so often they quickly learned that it was no good getting off the ferry and then hoping to get a lift. They prowled the deck during the crossing chatting up passengers, looking for lifts. 'A guy who would agree on the boat to give you a lift is the same guy who would pass you on the road side,' said Davies.

They never bought newspapers. 'They're in these yellow boxes,' Mick Jones said to me one day in Dunedin. 'It's much more fun over here. You just help yourself. That way they don't cost anything.'

The biggest problem for the bludgers was to get into grounds without paying and get decent seats. Mick was far and away the best at this. Out of twenty-two games he got away with paying only for seven.

'I use what little brains I've got,' explains Mick Jones. 'It was easiest at Westport. I just climbed over a piece of string. Don't forget you've come to a country that has never seen a crowd of 20 000 in the last six years. They haven't a clue how to handle us.'

'The easiest way is to look intently at something three miles away over in the hills and then just to head straight in when they are distracted. Saturday at Carisbrook was a classic,' continued Pat Collins, who was, with Mick, the most artful dodger. 'We got our tickets and got in. My ticket was for a terrible seat and there was no way I was going to sit there. I couldn't see anything. So I ended up with Mick in front of the main stand, eyeing the seats. We always looked in the main stands because there are always empty seats at every game, even Test matches. So there we were standing looking and a policeman came up to us and said "What are you two doing?"

"Looking for friends," we replied. This was just before kick off so we said: right, as soon as the teams come out on the pitch and everybody starts to settle down including the ushers and officials, then we go in and str.: ght up. Like Mick says all you've got to do is look as if you own the place and if you look determined enough they won't even bother you. If they say anything like, "Can I help you sir?" you say, "No, it's all right. I'm just on my way up there." You stand in the aisle for a moment and as soon as the ushers start sitting down you sit down.'

There was no end to their roguery. Jones and Collins had another trick for getting into a ground without paying. 'Just turn up five minutes before kick-off when the last minute rush is on. Eden Park in Auckland is a joke,' snorted Mick. 'For the Maori game I just walked through the turnstile and the bloke obviously had his foot on the turnstile control all the time. I was going to do the Twickenham bludge – it is always a quid at Twickenham, though it might have gone up now – and I had two dollars in my hand, ready. I was just going to give him the money when he let me through instead of putting the bar up. So I kept my money and ran. Even in Auckland where they are a bit brighter than in the rest of the country they are still a bit dopey.'

Despite these nefarious skills there were occasions when even the most artful bludger had to pay up. Even then there were ways of reducing the cost. At Westport four of them booked accommodation at a motor camp resort – and later another four sneaked in to join them. That way the total bill of NZ$20 (£11.70) was split between eight instead of four.

The one thing the young buccaneers had in common with the tour party supporters was that they both thought the Lions did a very bad job socially. 'We were disappointed with the reception we got from the team,' says Tony Clemo who ran one tour party of 125 people and was helped by former Lion Barry John. 'After all we had come to help the Lions. If you are a Lion on tour you expect to have to meet people, don't you?'

Carwyn James, the 1971 British Lions coach, and Dr Doug

Smith, the manager of that same team, were leading another, much smaller party. There could have been no greater contrast between the hitch-hikers and the tour groups than in Auckland at the end of the tour. Clemo's Red Dragon travel party stayed in the Intercontinental. Two miles away across town, Bird, Davies and friends were sleeping on the floor of an upstairs room of a pub owned by Ces Williams, the brother of the great All Black Bryan. And they were delighted to be there.

Chapter 19

George Burrell: a players' manager

The day before the third Test in Dunedin manager George Burrell issued stern orders to the hotel switchboard: no telephone calls to be put through to the players after 8 in the evening and before 10 the next morning. Burrell was worried that on the eve of the crucial Test his players would be disturbed by calls from well-meaning Welsh supporters who had flown in from Britain the previous day.

This was characteristic of Burrell who always wanted to protect and shield his players from the outside world. It was later suggested to him that this was a contributing reason for the accusations of standoffishness that were levelled at the Lions throughout the tour. New Zealanders and Britons alike criticized the 1977 Lions for not fulfilling their social duties.

An example occurred on the morning of 11 August when the Lions were due to leave for training straight after breakfast. It had been arranged that they would go to East Tamaki RFC in Auckland, a dozen miles or so from their hotel. The players gathered in the hall with their training bags while the coach waited on the yellow no parking lines outside.

George Burrell and John Dawes were missing and so were the liaison men. Upstairs in Burrell's room an argument was raging. The Lions' management were asking that the training be moved to Eden Park where the Test would be played in two days. Burrell wanted to spare his men an hour-long coach ride and to give them a chance to get more of a feeling for the ground. Another reason was to get the training session out of the way as quickly as possible so the team could do their shopping.

The liaison men, however, were insisting that the venue could not be changed so late in the day. They pointed out that club officials had been preparing for the Lions' visit for several days and the women had begun making cakes. Some local schools had granted their pupils a half-holiday to watch the training. In the end Burrell had to give in. His position was untenable, particularly since early in the tour he had agreed to the arrangements. But he only gave in reluctantly, and he and the team arrived at the ground in a sour mood.

In front of 2000 spectators the Lions trained, changed and went into the club-house where a feast was awaiting them. The local club officials regarded it as an honour to entertain the Lions and their pride was obvious. The players sat in a semi-circle with their backs to the centre of the room, talking to one another while eating their cream cakes, doughnuts and sandwiches, and drinking tea. After ten minutes they got up and left with the most cursory farewells. I could see the disappointment of club members and couldn't blame them for feeling that the Lions were standoffish. This was not the only example of the Lions offending their hosts with a simple discourtesy that ought to have been remedied.

Since the behaviour of the Lions was a reflection of the manager it was a criticism of Burrell that he was too weak with his men and let them get away with too much. Burrell was a players' manager and when in doubt over which course to follow he would always choose the one that would please the players.

As outside criticism that he didn't attempt to make the Lions more sociable increased, Burrell said very feebly, 'It is absolute nonsense to say the Lions were not sociable. All touring teams tend to sit by themselves after a game. This happens when we receive teams at home. Why couldn't other people have gone and mixed with the Lions? We have not turned down one invitation to go out and visit a hospital for instance or a school or an old people's home or an ex-wounded soldiers home. For me these are the important parts of being sociable on tour.'

Phil Bennett made an unscheduled visit to a hospital to see a man who had just had a leg amputated and had asked if he could see the Lions' captain. When a blind lady turned up at their hotel in Hamilton, the Lions seemed to have all the patience in the world to talk to her.

But were these admirable, spontaneous gestures enough or

were they exceptions that proved the general rule? The warmth
of the Lions' friendliness was felt by too few and their reluctance
to mix can partly be blamed for much of the hostility towards
them. Some of the Scots who had toured New Zealand two years
earlier found the world of difference between the warmth with
which they were received then and the hostility that surrounded
this tour. Perhaps Burrell, sensing the change in opinion, was
subconsciously reacting against it. Anyway, it was a very bad
mistake in one so experienced.

He was a real Scot, a man of set habits who didn't easily waver
from what he thought was right. In certain matters he was as
stubborn as a goat. Back home in Gala he gets up at 6.45 each
morning, leaves home at 8.15 and is always at his desk at the BP
office in Old St Boswells by 8.30. He liked to bring the same
order to his daily routine in New Zealand.

Before a match, nerves would keep him awake all night. But
whether he slept well or not he would be up early, have a quick
cup of coffee and one piece of toast for breakfast and then sit
down with his secretary Alex McDonald to handle the fifteen or
twenty letters he received each day. The letters were a mixture
of fan mail, administration and requests for the Lions to appear
or visit this school or that club.

This done he went to training, as much to see what was
happening as to get away from the telephone which he found a
menace. He was never so happy as at Taumarunui near the start
of the tour where he had no phone in his room.

The remaining time before lunch would be spent doing more
administration. Each afternoon he tried to snatch an hour's
sleep though he also made the most of the opportunities to go
jet-boating and sight-seeing that were offered to the team. He
was, however, a rare Scot in that he did not play golf. Even at
night he had little peace for there were friends to see, rugby men
to talk to and between fifteen and twenty phone calls to answer.

Burrell also had to look after a host of miscellanea all neatly
documented on an inventory from the Four Home Unions
Tours Committee. They included: 10 000 Lions badges which
the players handed out, 80 Lions ties to be presented to referees
and opposition captains, 32 Lions shields, 29 Lions pennants, 5
sets of jerseys and 2 sets of numbered substitute jerseys (jerseys
numbered 16–21), 10 spare jerseys, 19 spare numbers, 30 pairs

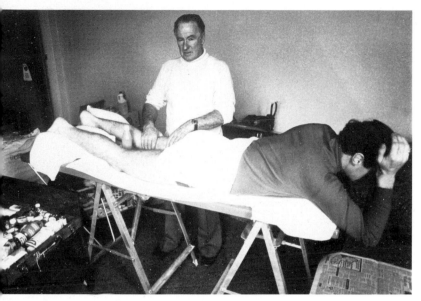

Doc Murdoch at work while Mike Gibson reads.
Baggage-man cum masseur, Doc never seemed to stop.

'Now look here Prime Minister,' says the author. Mr
Muldoon remains stony-faced.

'In classrooms I'm the one who's supposed to crack jokes,' says Ian McGeechan scratching his head. Bruce Hay and Doug Morgan enjoy the joke.

Andy Irvine signed more autographs than any other Lion and he never refused. Certainly not pretty young girls.

This was a rugby tour, but when rain drove them inside Trevor Evans showed he is no threat to Geoff Boycott.

Volleyball is easy if you have a 6 ft 5 in. player like Gordon Brown on your side. Fenwick, Cobner, Morgan, Rees all agree.

Tooting his horn rather than drowning his sorrows, a Lions supporter.
Left: The biggest leek in the land, even carried by a Welshman 12 000 miles from home, couldn't help the Lions in the first Test.

And they won, and they won! And how British supporters enjoyed watching the victory at the cavern without a soul — Lancaster Park.

of white shorts, 64 pairs of stockings, spare buttons (large and small), a number of team photos, 1000 sheets of headed note-paper and envelopes, and 600 thank you cards and envelopes.

The four home unions gave him an allowance of £1500 to pay for items such as telephone calls home to Britain, postage stamps and any expenses he incurred on rugby business in New Zealand that were not covered by the NZRFU. As an example, the cocktail party he gave before the team left for Fiji on their way home was paid out of his tour fund.

Burrell claimed he held more press conferences than any other Lions manager. In the main though, they were models of non-information, the news being handed out in the barest form and fewest words. He was asked once, for example, 'Were you upset that the injury Doug Morgan received against King Country – Wanganui was the result of what was blatantly a late tackle?'

'I am always upset when a player is injured. It is up to the referee to decide right from wrong,' was his full reply to a question about an incident that could have ended in a player being invalided home.

I remember asking him just before the second Test whether Terry Cobner had been on the selection committee. 'He helped us,' Burrell replied cautiously.

'But was he on the committee? Did he attend the meeting?' I asked.

'I am not prepared to answer that.' One heard time and again that rather abrupt sentence with its ring of finality.

Privately in his room or at the bar his traditional Scottish reserve towards the press faded and he was much more frank and helpful.

Burrell had come a long way in rugby since he won his international caps as a full back for Scotland twenty-five years ago. When he stopped playing he took up refereeing and soon graduated to the international panel. His first experience of touring came on Scotland's short trip to Australia in 1970 when as assistant manager he had to take over unexpectedly from Hector Monro, MP, who was called back to fight a General Election.

In 1975 Burrell was made manager of Scotland's five-week tour of New Zealand and his success then made him the obvious front-runner for the Lions' job. After the appointments for New Zealand were made the rugby journalists gave a lunch for Burrell and Dawes. In a tweedy suit and sturdy shoes Burrell looked every bit the alickadoo. 'We shall look for forwards who can get possession and backs who can do the simple things at speed,' he said bravely. 'Win the ball, win the game. That is our motto.' This motto, had he been reminded of it, would probably have haunted him in the last stage of the tour. In both the third and fourth Tests the Lions did win the ball, only to lose both games.

At the end of the tour I asked him whether it had been harder than he expected. 'Much harder,' he replied. 'I knew it was going to be more difficult than the Scottish tour of two years ago but never, ever, as hard as it turned out to be. The pressures from the media, from commercial interests, let alone from playing, are huge. I think there is far too much at stake now. People are living like lice on the players' backs and I don't like it. I am upset at the amount of commercialism surrounding this tour. I don't want or expect my players to get anything out of it but it annoys me that others are exploiting them.

'There are so many people who want to latch on to the Lions – social secretaries of a Rotary Club, Junior Chambers of Commerce. All these types of things. I think it is a feather in a hat of a social secretary if he can get one or two Lions along and one or two of the management. These requests may not seem much but they are all time-consuming and quite a strain on the players.'

He and John Dawes shared a protective paranoia about their team. Their sensitivity to criticism from the press was understandable perhaps, but they also remained very aloof when the management of the 1971 Lions, Dr Doug Smith and Carwyn James, arrived in New Zealand with a party of supporters for the last three weeks of the tour. They did not like to be reminded of the former victorious teams. A photograph of some 1971 Lions was once produced and shown around. When Burrell saw it he snarled quite uncharacteristically, 'Put that bloody thing away.'

'There was only one thing we were expected to do and that was to win,' said Burrell at the end of the tour. 'We were on to a hiding to nothing and no touring team has ever been under such strain.'

There were moments when it looked as though Burrell would crack under the enormous, unrelenting pressure. Yet he somehow pulled through. There was a lot of talk throughout the tour as to how many Lions would return to New Zealand. Nobody thought to ask George Burrell. So would he go back? He smiled and kept his silence. Was there an echo of a familiar phrase, 'I am not prepared to answer that'?

Chapter 20

Fourth Test – Lions 9 All Blacks 10

There were a lot of tears shed in the Lions dressing room at Eden Park Auckland on 13 August. They couldn't believe they had thrown away a victory that everybody thought should have been theirs. For more than half the game it looked as though the Lions were going to win and level the series, two Tests each.

But then Mother Fortune dealt them a stroke of bad luck and the All Blacks snatched a victory they didn't deserve and won the series.

Once again the All Blacks forwards were made to look wan and ineffectual by the powerful Lions eight, just as had happened at Christchurch a month earlier. It didn't matter that both Terry Cobner and Derek Quinnell were not fit to play in the fourth Test. Cobner had torn a hamstring in his leg the previous Saturday in the same game as Derek Quinnell broke a bone in his left hand.

Their replacements were Tony Neary, the Englishman whose play had improved so much in the previous month that he was very close to ousting Cobner from the Test team anyway, and Jeff Squire. Neary took over the pack leadership as well. Squire had more physical presence at the line out than Trevor Evans, the only other candidate for Quinnell's place. Squire's dramatic improvement since arriving at Gisborne in the third week of the tour somehow personified the improvement by the Lions forwards.

Even with these two changes the Lions forwards were still too powerful for the All Blacks. The front five of Price, Wheeler and Cotton, Beaumont and Brown, who had played together since the second Test, were truly magnificent in their scrummaging. Kent Lambert's return at tight head prop for the All Blacks helped but did not give the New Zealand front row parity in strength.

With his scrum under enormous pressure and the line out work less tidy than it should have been, scrum half Lyn Davis had a rough afternoon. He managed to clear the ball surprisingly well yet he was still caught occasionally by Doug Morgan. The lack of protection for Davis meant he was a moment slower than he should have been; that, in turn, meant that Doug Bruce was caught by Tony Neary more often than he should have been.

Far from this Test being the Becher's Brook for the Lions it has always seemed to previous Lions sides (since the war only the 1959 Lions have won the fourth Test in New Zealand), the Lions began by cocking a snook at history. They started with imposition and majesty, taking the game to the All Blacks just as so many sides had battered and rammed them in the opening minutes of their previous twenty-four matches.

The playing of Doug Morgan at scrum half meant that the ball was nearly always going to go back in front of the forwards. Morgan, with a short and not very quick pass, is a kicking scrum half – just what was needed for this Test. If he didn't kick then Bennett did.

For sixty minutes the Lions were almost in complete control and they led 9–3. Bevan Wilson, the All Black full back, had kicked one penalty for the All Blacks. Doug Morgan had kicked one and scored and converted his own try. The try was a good one coming after sustained pressure followed a prearranged move by the forwards.

It began with Cotton running from the front to the back of the line out to catch a ball tapped down to him. Cotton passed it to his Lancashire team-mate Beaumont who made a few yards and then passed to Graham Price outside him. By now play was nearly in front of the All Blacks posts twenty yards out. Price linked with Fenwick and when the centre was tackled he got the ball back quickly. Seizing his chance for glory, Morgan continued the left to right movement of the ball by picking it up and diving for the All Blacks' line.

At dinner with some friends earlier in the week Morgan had been surprised when a stranger stopped and said to him, 'I'm a

New Zealander and I hope for our sake that you're not playing
on Saturday,' before walking away. Rather taken aback, Morgan
muttered, 'Thanks very much.'

There had been speculation that the Scot would be dropped
in favour of Welshman Alun Lewis who had a very long quick
pass. Lewis came out from England to replace Brynmor Williams when Williams's hamstring finally gave out in the third
Test. Within two days the ebullient Welshman was thrown in
against Sid Going and three days after that he played again. But
Morgan was preferred for the Test match.

The pattern of aggressive forward play by the British continued until the last quarter of the Test when at last the All Blacks
managed to generate some of the form that All Blacks are
supposed to inherit. Tane Norton took a strike against the head.
Bryan Williams was cleverly released on the blind side, and ten
yards from his own line toed the ball after being tackled. Phil
Bennett, covering across from deep midfield, oddly missed the
ball and it rolled into touch as Andy Irvine and Williams
approached it at high speed and from different directions.

Such moments clearly heralded something. As the Lions let
loose their grip on the game and moved the ball more, so the All
Blacks were able to claw their way back into the game. Bevan
Wilson landed his second penalty after a Lion had put a hand
into a scrum. Three minutes later Wilson missed another 30-
yarder this time from the right field. He probably thought that
he had failed to level the game for the All Blacks. With five
minutes left the Lions seemed destined to make history by
becoming the first Lions side since the Second War to come
from behind and level a Test series.

They had beaten the All Blacks forwards into submission, put
the ball back in front of the forwards and, when they did move it,
they cut out most of those nail-biting errors they were prone to
make.

Bennett was late-tackled. A penalty and up stepped Morgan.
This was the moment the little Scotsman could live off for ever if
he converted it. He placed the ball carefully 30 yards out,
slightly to the right of the posts. He had 98 points to his credit so
far on tour. This was to be his last chance to join Phil Bennett as
the only Lions to score more than 100 points.

The ball slid agonizingly left of the posts. It wasn't a difficult kick; yet with a 3-point lead and only a few minutes of injury time left Morgan couldn't have been too disappointed.

The game entered injury time as Phil Bennett ran back to field a speculative kick ahead. He took two steps infield, shot for touch and missed. Bill Osborne gathered the ball and punted it down towards the Lions' left corner where Fenwick fielded it, half turning as he did so. Osborne caught him with a fierce tackle, jolting him as he passed to Wheeler. The hooker was tackled equally hard by Mourie and the ball was jolted out of his hands too. Lawrie Knight, the tall No. 8, grabbed it and raced over to dive flamboyantly in the corner.

The partisan crowd went wild, of course. Papers shot up in the air, cushions too, and hats. The Lions suddenly looked exhausted, the forwards sickened. Had they lost? Surely not, not after all they had done. But they had. They bravely took play to the All Blacks line and first at a line out and then at a scrum they thought they had scored.

In the end they moved the ball from the set scrum. Andy Irvine came into the line but knocked the ball on. How sadly apposite that the last move of the tour should have been bungled. How often had that happened on tour?

'We out-scrummaged, out-jumped, out-everythinged them, yet we lost the game,' said a sad George Burrell. 'They were out-thought, out-fought and out-played,' added an equally sad-looking Dawes. The All Blacks had won the game 10-9, the series 3-1, had outscored the Lions by 6 tries to 3 and 54 to 41 points. The All Blacks had won to mark what they hoped was the start of another era in New Zealand rugby history. The New Zealand three quarters existed on less ball than the Lions' backs – and used it better. They discovered an outstanding full back in Bevan Wilson, who was an adequate goal kicker. And as British teams have been doing in New Zealand for years, the New Zealand team overcame the handicap of their forwards being badly beaten in scrums and line outs.

John Dawes wanted to do the tour his way. The players were his men, and it was Dawes rather than manager Burrell who emerged as the stronger personality. So the final judgement on the 1977 British Lions centres on the part played by the 37-year-old Welshman.

The tour was a failure if it is judged by the ultimate yardstick of the Test series. The Lions didn't produce their potential and they lost to an ill-balanced and unproven All Black team. Dawes held his dream that he could win his 100 days war by playing flowing rugby, the style he had always favoured. But when it was clear there was something wrong with his three quarters it appeared to me that he seemed confused and unable to remedy the fault. How strange this was when he had been an outstanding centre himself.

At first the Lions backs started brilliantly, with their running and handling at Wairarapa-Bush in foul conditions. At King Country–Wanganui they scored eight tries, Andy Irvine getting five, J.J. Williams two and Phil Bennett one. Slowly though, things began to go wrong.

The brilliance that had been promised at the start only flashed occasionally now. At Southland Andy Irvine showed two touches of class, and Elgan Rees and Gareth Evans were able to score tries as a result. But then things got worse. The alignment of the backs seemed skew whiff. They looked to be over-anxious, and the more over-anxious they became the more mistakes they made. The third Test was the nadir for British back play. Had there ever been a worse demonstration? By the end of the tour it was becoming an event when they managed to pass the ball down the line without dropping it.

This was the time when Dawes should have ordered more practice, even though it was getting a bit late. Did the extremely promising wing Elgan Rees get the attention someone so young and inexperienced needed? Clinics may be associated with Carwyn James and 1971, but why didn't Dawes introduce something similar?

John Dawes was not an easy man to get to know. He could be very friendly, articulate, helpful. And sometimes if you crossed him he would be contrite afterwards. Yet he could also harbour a grudge for a lòng time.

He spent many hours on tour arguing with journalists who had criticized him or his players. Too often the arguments became so heated that all rhyme and reason went out of the window. There were times when one wished that Dawes would spend as much time practising and coaching the three quarters as he would defending them.

The way Dawes attacked critics of him or his players made it seem that he took his rugby more seriously than almost anything else. Yet one of his catch phrases was, 'Never mind, it's only a game.'

'Sure it's only a game,' says Jack Gleeson, the All Blacks coach, 'and I do understand what he means when he says that and to a degree it is true. I am speaking to you, I am alive and well, I have not got cancer – I hope. Sure it is only a game but it is a game that everyone wants to win.'

I travelled with John Dawes for three and a half months in New Zealand, played squash with him, drank with him and talked and talked with him. However, I don't know him any better now than I did before. I had a tongue-lashing from him once, and we had a real stand-up, scratch-your-eyes-out fight another time. Power is a word he used a lot in New Zealand. 'You have no power,' he would say to journalists. 'I have power.'

There were many unforeseeable reasons that made things more difficult for Dawes. The team suffered a spate of injuries, an onslaught from several New Zealand newspapers and the bad weather depressed everyone. It will go down in history as The Bad News Tour.

I personally believe though that one of the most important reasons why the Lions failed was because John Dawes would not believe that his way of doing things was not the right way. Like Frank Sinatra, Dawes did it his way, and I believe that his way was wrong.

Chapter 21

Norton's nirvana

Tane Norton stood encircled by jubilant New Zealand spectators cheering and singing Auld Lang Syne. He was busy
savouring the applause of the crowd and what had just gone
before was only slowly sinking in. Norton had achieved what no
other All Black captain had managed in this decade. He had led
the All Blacks to victory in a major Test, following defeats by
South Africa in 1970 and 1976 and the British Lions in 1971.
Now he leaned over the front of the main stand at Eden Park,
Auckland, a black track suit top over his All Black jersey, a towel
wrapped around his neck. By his side stood Phil Bennett,
captain of the defeated Lions, wiping tears of disappointment
away from his eyes.

Moments earlier Norton's team had stolen a cheeky victory
over the Lions. After trailing for most of the game during which
the Lions looked the certain winners, the All Blacks scored a try
in injury time and won 10-9. That victory gave them a 3-1 result
in the series against the Lions.

The New Zealand crowd was ecstatic. 'Hell's bells, it was
tremendous to see all those people standing down on the field
and it was only then that it really sank that we had won,' said
Norton later. 'I thought they would have all rushed·off to the
pub.'

Two months earlier when he was appointed captain of the All
Blacks he could only have wished for such scenes. The morning
after his appointment I rang him. I had never met him, and I
wasn't sure what his reaction would be to a complete stranger
disturbing him at seven in the morning. As it happened he was
already up and about the house. Mind you it could hardly have

been otherwise as he has four rumbustious boys aged between one and ten. For them this morning was no different from any other as they weren't old enough to appreciate their father's moment of glory. 'At breakfast one had a headache, another had a sore stomach and the third was going around thumping everything in sight. Nobody congratulated me or said anything to me at all,' said Norton.

'Can I come up and see you today?' I asked.

'Sure,' he replied. 'Come on up later on.'

We met him in his office in the centre of Christchurch. He was a tall man, slim with black hair and a moustache, and he was wearing a brown leather jacket. He forecast that both the All Blacks and the Lions would play a similar style of rugby in the Tests. 'In Test matches the only difference between teams tends to be in the colour of the jerseys they are wearing,' he said.

As it happened the opposite was true. As the series went on it became clear that the All Blacks had the better backs and therefore wanted every opportunity to unleash them. The Lions' forwards were stronger than the All Blacks. The British therefore tried to close the game up, to keep the ball in front of their forwards as much as possible. This was particularly so at Christchurch in the last twenty minutes of the second Test.

There were hints of changes in the traditional strengths of British and New Zealand rugby at Wellington and Christchurch in the first two Tests. The real emergence of the All Blacks backs as powerful runners however, came in the third Test. At the same time the Lions showed convincingly that their forwards could shove back the All Blacks in set scrums and dominate them in the line out.

In the Test series Norton did a difficult job well. From the position of hooker he proved an able leader of the All Blacks. He seemed to overcome the problems of being last man up from set scrums by having communication with his backs through stand off Doug Bruce, his Canterbury team-mate. 'No captain ever wins a series on his own,' Norton told me when we met first. 'That is the team's job. The captain's job is to have communication, no matter where you are in a team. If you captain from first five-eighth [stand off] then you are relying on certain players in key positions to tell you what is happening. Then you say, "Do this, do that." ' Norton always remembers being told by an old and wise coach when he was young, 'Never forget you can't win the ball without the rest of the team.'

Captaincy of the All Blacks came to him rather late. In fact one thing that characterizes Norton's rugby career is that everything has come to him later rather than sooner. In his case the wait seems to be for seven years. He first played representative rugby as an 18-year-old in 1961. Then he was dropped until 1968. In 1970, aged 27, he made the first of his twenty-seven Test appearances and seven years later he was made captain. As if by way of preparation for this promotion, he led the All Blacks in three matches in South Africa in 1976. In the first Test against the Lions he equalled hooker Bruce McLeod's record of twenty-four successive Tests.

Norton was born in Methven, a town fifty miles east of Christchurch, on 30 March 1943. His ancestors on his mother's side were Maori. His christian names Rangitane and Will are naturally Maori. In Maorio *rangi* means father figure and *tane*, pronounced *ta-knee*, means man. Thirty-four in March 1977, Norton was the oldest All Black to play against the Lions in 1977, older even than Sid Going. He was the Rangitane of the team. His second name, Will, is after his father's brother who was killed in Gallipoli, aged 19, in the First World War.

To meet for the first time Norton is friendly and jovial. He seemed at ease with strangers and it is easy to see why he was made captain. He works for a life insurance company and lives with his wife Jacky and their children in a Christchurch suburb called Opawa. Norton's one-storey house is filled with plaques, pennants and badges marking games in his career. I noticed the shields from Tonga, Neath, Australia and Aberavon on one wall. Overlooking the house are the Cashmere Hills where he does his pre-season training.

We drove up into these same hills to take some photographs of him in his All Black strip. He pointed out a sheep limping badly on the hillside opposite where we were standing. 'There's a dog roaming about that chases the sheep,' he said. 'It chases them over the edge of the gulches and then gnaws the carcass when the sheep are dead. A friend of mine has lost four or five sheep that way this year. Sometimes I go out with him to try and shoot the dog but we haven't found him yet.'

We spent an hour photographing Norton and had a lot of fun.

The ground was muddy and in some places water flowed across our paths. As Sir Walter Raleigh spread his cloak over a puddle so that Queen Elizabeth would not get her feet wet, so Norton, who was wearing his rugby boots, insisted on carrying both Adrian Murrell and myself over the watery parts to save our flimsy town shoes.

The night before he had played for Canterbury, his province, against the New Zealand Universities at Lancaster Park. He was standing in the bar after the game when he heard of his appointment as captain. 'I am glad it is all over – the captaincy thing,' he said later. 'There had been a lot of paper talk and a lot of pressure. I felt sorry for Graham Mourie' [who had captained the Junior All Blacks in Argentina and had seemed the logical successor to the former All Black captain Andy Leslie].

We talked about the demands of captaincy, the responsibility and extra pressure he was under now. It would take up a lot of time. He hadn't done any work that morning and he wouldn't get much done that afternoon either.

'It is a problem for a self-employed person like me,' Norton admitted. 'When I went away before, I was paid. Now I am not. I have the use of an office and a telephone but I have to travel a lot seeing clients. I work on commission. I thought a long time before I left the bank [of New Zealand] last year but then I decided I wanted to be on my own. I resigned before going to South Africa with the All Blacks. I didn't think it would be fair to leave straight after I came back home from the tour. I still go back to the bank. I still have an overdraft – I guess they must still like me.'

By now it was three o'clock and there was an autumnal sharpness in the air. We drove down from the hills. 'I have to try and find another house,' said Norton as we passed some big houses set back from the road. 'Ours is getting too small.'

'In another area or still around here?' I asked.

'Around here. I like it here.'

We arrived back at his house. His sand-coloured Triumph 2500 was in the drive. He invited us in for a cup of tea and we would have liked to stay, but unfortunately we had to catch a plane.

'Thank you very much for all the time you gave us,' I said. I hadn't really expected that after talking to us for an hour in his office he would agree to spend a further two hours being photographed up in the hills. But then I hadn't expected him to be such an obliging person.

'That's OK,' he said as he shut the door of the car. 'You got in first so you were lucky. I wouldn't do that for everyone. Come to think of it,' he added, 'I wouldn't do it for anyone else.' With a smile he went back into his house.

Chapter 22

Fiji: *Bula, Bula, Bula*

'I tell you what,' said Fran Cotton as he piled his plate with cucumber, beans and potato salad before queuing for his two barbecued steaks. 'They've got this tour wrong. It should have been fourteen weeks here and three days in New Zealand.'

To spend three days on sunny Pacific islands like Fiji on their way back to London was a very welcome bonus for the players at the end of the tour. And as the warm evening air rushed in through the glassless windows of the rickety airport bus it seemed to blow away all the tensions and worries that had built up over the previous three and a half months.

At Nandi airport there had been lots of happy, smiling faces to welcome the Lions, all waiting to shake hands and say, *'Bula, Bula'* [hello]. To have the British Lions touring team on their island was a great honour for the rugby-mad local population. For the first time ever the Fijian national team would play the Lions and the *Fiji Times* even suggested their men had a chance to win.

By nine o'clock on match day there were 200 spectators strung around the pitch at Buckhurst Park, Suva. At the kick off 20 000 smiling, chattering and giggling Fijians had squeezed into the ground and several hundred more were perched on palm trees overlooking the picturesque ground.

The Lions played badly. The excitement in the crowd built up as the highly-trained Fijians beat their distinguished visitors 25–21. The real winner was the referee who awarded the Lions only three penalties in the first half and just one in the second while showering his countrymen with eight in the first half and eleven in the second.

The Lions took it good-humouredly. Later that night a very

pretty girl said to a Lion, 'Wouldn't you like to meet my brother? He is very famous you know. He refereed your game today.'

'Not tonight darling. Tomorrow perhaps,' was the slightly huffy reply.

There was an official party and cabaret that night and after a Fijian choir had sung beautifully it was the Lions' turn to entertain their hosts. They gave a rendering of their team song *Country Road* which was followed by some more singing by the Fijians. The Lions were invited to reply once again but this time they declined. 'We're two nil down already,' said Ian McGeechan drily. 'That's enough for one day.'

Wednesday was spent shopping and the Lions prowled around the markets and shops of Suva in search of presents to take home. There were voodoo masks in rainwood, baskets and colourful beads and bracelets made from local seeds.

The Lions relished the opportunity to bargain with shrewd Indian shopkeepers. Trevor Evans was particularly good at it. He would open his invariably successful bargaining by saying, 'Now look here, you're so rich they tell me that you fly home to India every week-end.'

In this duty-free paradise the Lions got quite carried away and their plane was much heavier when they took off that Wednesday evening.

The difficulties that had dogged The Bad News Tour stuck with the Lions to the end. A strike at London airport disrupted air traffic throughout the world, and by the time the Lions landed twelve hours late on Friday morning they had been thirty-six hours on their journey around the world getting diverted to Seattle and Copenhagen.

The plane was so late arriving that the planned reception for the Lions had to be cancelled and the reporters and photographers went home. But the wives still waited. And there were three men in track suits from Llanelli rugby club who eagerly awaited the arrival of a Lions rugby ball. As if it were the Olympic flame they were going to run with it to Llanelli for charity. Within minutes of the plane touching down the Lions had collected their baggage. At 2.55 on Friday 19 August 1977 they walked past customs and into the arrivals hall. Their tour was over.

The matches

Match 1:   British Isles *v.* Wairapa-Bush
Masterton, 18 May
British Isles 41   Wairapa-Bush 13

British Isles
Hay (rep. Irvine); Squires, McGeechan, Burcher, J.J. Williams;
Bennett (Capt.), B. Williams; No. 8 Quinnell; T. Evans, Horton (rep.
Duggan), Keane, Cobner; Orr, Wheeler, Price
Tries: Squires, J.J. Williams (3), Burcher (2), Cobner (2)
Conversions: Bennett (3)
Penalty: Bennett

Wairapa-Bush
N. Kjestrup; C. Paton, B. Patrick, K. England; H. Huriwai, A.
O'Neill, B. Herangi; N. Taylor; I. Turley, B. Clarke (rep. J. Darling-
ton), P. Guscott, P. Mahoney; N. Sargent, G. McGlashan, B. Row-
lands (Capt.)
Tries: McGlashan, Paton
Conversion: Kjestrup
Penalty: Kjestrup

Referee: A. Taylor (Canterbury)

Match 2:   British Isles *v.* Hawke's Bay
Napier, 21 May
British Isles 13   Hawke's Bay 11

British Isles
Irvine; J.J. Williams, Fenwick, Gibson, G. Evans; Bevan, Morgan;
No. 8 Duggan; Neary, Brown, Martin, Quinnell; C. Williams, Wind-
sor, Cotton (Capt.)
Try: Irvine
Penalties: Fenwick (3)

Hawke's Bay
M. Tocker; P. Durham, R. Allen, K. Taylor; R. Bremner (rep. W. Nixon); H. Paewai; J. McCarroll; P. Ryan; T. Carter, R. Stuart (Capt.), M.McCool, J. Paraha; B. Dunstan, I. Grant, J.O'Connor
Tries: Stuart, Taylor
Penalty: Tocker

Referee: W. Adlam (Wanganui)

Match 3:   British Isles *v.* Poverty Bay–East Coast
Gisborne, 25 May
British Isles 25   Poverty Bay–East Coast 6

British Isles
Hay (rep. Irvine); Squires, McGeechan (Capt), Gibson, G. Evans; Bevan, Morgan; No. 8 Duggan; Neary, Keane, Martin, T. Evans; C. Williams, Windsor, Cotton
Tries: McGeechan (2), G. Evans
Conversions: Morgan (2)
Penalties: Morgan (3)

Poverty Bay–East Coast
W. Isaac; J. Walters, B. Sherriff (rep. L. Richard), G. Torrie; M. Parkinson, G. Thompson; S. Donald; L. Knight; I. Kirkpatrick (Capt.), C. Kirkpatrick, B. Cameron, R. Falcon; R. Newlands, G. Allen, W. McFarlane
Penalties: Isaac (2)

Referee: M. Farnworth (Auckland)

Match 4:   British Isles *v.* Taranaki
New Plymouth, 28 May
British Isles 21   Taranaki 13

British Isles
Irvine; J.J. Williams, Fenwick, Burcher, G. Evans; Bennett (Capt.), B. Williams; No. 8 Quinnell; T. Evans, Brown, Horton, Cobner; Orr, Wheeler, Price
Tries: Irvine, J.J. Williams
Conversions: Irvine, Bennett
Penalties: Irvine (2), Bennett

Taranaki
S. Davidson; T. Brown, P. Wharehoka, J. O'Sullivan; B. Glading, P. Martin; D. Loveridge (rep. P. Fleming); M. Carey; G. Mourie (Capt.), I. Eliason, J. Thwaites, R. Fraser; B. McEldowney, F. O'Carroll, J. McEldowney

Try: O'Sullivan
Penalty: Martin
Drop goals: Martin (2)

Referee: P. McDavitt (Wellington)

Match 5: British Isles *v.* King Country-Wanganui
Taumarunui, 1 June
British Isles 60   King Country-Wanganui 9

British Isles
Irvine; J.J. Williams, Fenwick, McGeechan, Squires; Bennett
(Capt.), Morgan (rep. B. Williams); No. 8 Quinnell; Squire, Keane,
Martin, Neary; Orr, Wheeler, Cotton
Tries: Irvine (5), J.J. Williams (2), Bennett, Quinnell, Squire, B.
Williams
Conversions: Bennett (8)

King Country-Wanganui
F. Hill; R. Murray, M. Kidd, B. Donovan; B. Osborne, C. Howard; S.
Pye; J. Tarrant; R. Stafford (Capt.), G. Mitchison, G. Coleman, B.
Middleton; B. Dallinson, G. Potaka, G. Lethborg
Try: Snowden
Conversion: Hill
Penalty: Hill

Referee: J. Walker (Otago)

Match 6: British Isles *v.* Manawatu-Horowhenua
Palmerston North, 4 June
British Isles 18   Manawatu-Horowhenua 12

British Isles
Hay; G. Evans, Burcher, Fenwick, Squires; Bevan, B. Williams; No. 8
Duggan; Cobner (Capt.) (rep. Quinnell), Horton, Keane, Squire; C.
Williams, Windsor, Price
Tries: B. Williams, Fenwick, Hay, C. Williams
Conversion: Fenwick

Manawatu-Horowhenua
A. Innes; K. Granger, M. Nutting, M. Watts; D. Rollerson (Capt.), B.
Morris (rep. P. Broederlow); M. Donaldson; G. Old; K. Eveleigh, J.
Loveday (rep. G. Knight), J. Calleson, L. Robinson; K. Lambert, D.
Easton, P. Harris
Drop goal: Morris
Penalties: Rollerson (3)

Referee: T. Doocey (Canterbury)

Match 7:　British Isles *v.* Otago
Dunedin, 8 June
British Isles 12　Otago 7

British Isles
Irvine; Rees, Burcher, Gibson, J.J. Williams; Bennett (Capt.), B.
Williams; No. 8 Duggan; T. Evans, Martin, Horton (rep. Keane),
Squire; Cotton, Wheeler, Price
Penalties: Bennett (4)

Otago
B. Wilson; R. Gibson, G. Bennetts (rep. S. Thompson), J. Colling; D.
Colling, L. Jaffray; T. Burcher; M. Jaffray (Capt.); R. Smith, W.
Graham, G. Seear, R. Roy; L. Clark, K. Bloxham, R. O'Connell
Try: Wilson
Penalty: Wilson

Referee: B. Duffy (Taranaki)

Match 8:　British Isles *v.* Southland
Invercargill, 11 June
British Isles 20　Southland 12

British Isles
Hay (rep. Irvine); Rees, Gibson, McGeechan, G. Evans; Bennett
(Capt.), B. Williams; No. 8 Duggan; T. Evans, Martin, Brown,
Squire; Orr, Windsor, Price
Tries: Rees, G. Evans, Gibson
Conversion: Irvine
Penalties: Martin (2)

Southland
J. Gardiner; E. McLellan, W. Boynton, S. O'Donnell; S. Pokere, B.
McKechnie; D. Shanks; A. McGregor; L. Rutledge, F. Oliver
(Capt.), M. Leach, S. Anderson; D. Saunders, B. Lamb, P. Butt
Penalties: McKechnie (4)

Referee: J. Pring (Auckland)

Match 9:　British Isles *v.* New Zealand Universities
Christchurch, 14 June
British Isles 9　New Zealand Universities 21

British Isles
Hay; Squires, McGeechan (Capt.), Burcher, Rees; Bevan, Morgan;
No. 8 Quinnell; Squire, Keane (rep. Orr), Brown (rep. Martin),
Neary; C. Williams, Wheeler, Cotton

Try: Quinnell
Conversion: Morgan
Penalty: Morgan

New Zealand Universities
D. Heffernan; R. Scott, D. Fouhy, R. Hawkins; P. Macfie, D. Rollerson (Capt.); M. Romans; G. Elvin; R. Scott, G. Brown, W. Graham, D. Thorn; P. Oliver, D. Syms, G. Denholm
Try: Macfie
Conversion: Rollerson
Penalties: Rollerson (3), Heffernan (2)

Referee: K. Lynch (Poverty Bay)

Match 10:   British Isles *v.* New Zealand (First Test)
Wellington, 18 June
British Isles 12   New Zealand 16

British Isles
Irvine; Squires, Fenwick, McGeechan, J.J. Williams; Bennett (Capt.), B. Williams; No. 8 Duggan; Cobner, Martin, Keane, T. Evans; Orr, Windsor, Price
Penalties: Bennett (3), Irvine

New Zealand
C. Farrell; G. Batty, B. Robertson, B. Williams; B. Osborne, D. Robertson; S. Going; L. Knight; I. Kirkpatrick, A. Haden, F. Oliver, K. Eveleigh; B. Johnstone, T. Norton (Capt.), K. Lambert
Tries: Going, Johnstone, Batty
Conversions: Williams (2)

Referee: P. McDavitt (Wellington)

Match 11:   British Isles *v.* Hanan Shield Districts
Timaru, 22 June
British Isles 45   Hanan Shield Districts 6

British Isles
Irvine; Rees, Gibson, G. Evans, J. J. Williams; McGeechan, Morgan; No. 8 Quinnell; Neary, Martin, Beaumont, Cobner (Capt.); C. Williams, Wheeler, Cotton
Tries: Rees (2), J.J. Williams, G.·Evans, Wheeler, Irvine
Conversions: Irvine (6)
Penalties: Irvine (3)

Hanan Shield Districts
D. Nicol (rep. P. Keenan); L. Palmer, A. Grieve, B. Cooper; A.

McLaren, T. Goddard; P. Williams; H. King; P. Grant, B. Anderson (Capt.), J. Ross, N. Glass; B. Higginson, D. Sloper, G. Prendergast
Penalties: Nicol (2)

Referee: B. Williams (West Coast)

Match 12:   British Isles *v.* Canterbury
Christchurch, 25 June
British Isles 14   Canterbury 13

British Isles
Irvine; J.J. Williams, Fenwick, Burcher, G. Evans; Bevan, Morgan; No. 8 Duggan; T. Evans (rep. Squire), Brown, Martin, Cobner (Capt.); Orr, Windsor, Cotton
Tries: G. Evans, J.J. Williams
Penalties: Irvine (2)

Canterbury
D. Heffernan; R. Scott, A. Jefferd, S. Cartwright; M. McEwan, D. Bruce; L. Davis; A. Wyllie (Capt.) (rep. S. Purdon); J. Phillips, G. Higginson, V. Stewart, D. Thompson; B. Bush, T. Norton, J. Ashworth
Tries: Jefferd, Ashworth
Conversion: Heffernan
Penalty: Heffernan

Referee: D. Millar (Otago)

Match 13:   British Isles *v.* West Coast–Buller
Westport, 29 June
British Isles 45   West Coast–Buller 0

British Isles
Hay; Squires, Burcher, Gibson, Rees; Bevan, Morgan; No. 8 Squire; T. Evans (Capt.), Keane, Beaumont, Neary; C. Williams, Windsor, Cotton
Tries: Squires (2), Hay, Squire, Beaumont, Bevan, Morgan
Conversion: Morgan (4)
Penalties: Morgan (3)

West Coast–Buller
R. Mumm; P. Teen, B. Davidson, T. Mundy; B. Morgan, A. Ireland; J. Gilbert; B.McGuire; N. Roberts, J. Sullivan, J. Lee (Capt.), M. Sinclair; R. Banks, R. Mitchell, J. Steffens

Referee: G. Harrison (Wellington)

Match 14:   British Isles *v*. Wellington
Wellington, 2 July
British Isles 13   Wellington 6

British Isles
Irvine; G. Evans, McGeechan, Fenwick, J.J. Williams; Bennett (Capt.), B. Williams; No. 8 Quinnell; Neary, Martin, Brown, Cobner; Cotton, Wheeler, Price
Try: Cobner
Penalties: Bennett (3)

Wellington
C. Currie; W. Proctor, I. May, B. Fraser; R. Cleland, J. Dougan; D. Henderson; A. Leslie (Capt.); M. Stevens, B. Gardiner, J. Fleming, P. Quinn; K. Phelan, F. Walker, A. Keown
Penalties: Cleland (2)

Referee: C. Gregan (Waikato)

Match 15:   British Isles *v*. Marlborough–Nelson Bays
Blenheim, 5 July
British Isles 40   Marlborough–Nelson Bays 23

British Isles
Hay; Rees, Burcher, Gibson, Squires; Bevan, Morgan (rep. B. Williams); No. 8 Squire; Quinnell, Brown, Beaumont, T. Evans (Capt.); C. Williams, Windsor, Price (rep. Orr)
Tries: Hay, Burcher, Rees, B. Williams, Brown
Conversions: Gibson (2), Morgan (2)
Penalties: Morgan (2), Gibson (2)

Marlborough–Nelson Bays
R. Gordon; B. Hunter, S. Marfell, B. Ford; G. Rogers, J. Speedy; P. Baker; B. Kenny; D. Neal, M. West, T. Julian (Capt.), M. Best; J. Baryluk, K. Sutherland, G. Paki Paki
Tries: Rogers (2)
Penalties: Marfell (5)

Referee: N. Whittaker (Manawatu)

Match 16:   British Isles *v*. New Zealand (Second Test)
Christchurch, 9 July
British Isles 13   New Zealand 9

British Isles
Irvine; J.J. Williams, McGeechan, Fenwick, G. Evans; Bennett (Capt.), B. Williams; No. 8 Duggan; Quinnell, Brown, Beaumont, Cobner; Cotton, Wheeler, Price

Try: J.J. Williams
Penalties: Bennett (3)

New Zealand
C. Farrell; B. Williams, B. Osborne, M. Taylor; L. Jaffray, D. Bruce; S. Going; L. Knight; K. Eveleigh, F. Oliver, A. Haden, I. Kirkpatrick; B. Johnstone, T. Norton (Capt.), B. Bush
Penalties: Williams (3)

Referee: B. Duffy (Taranaki)

Match 17:   British Isles *v*. New Zealand Maoris
Auckland, 13 July
British Isles 22   New Zealand Maoris 19

British Isles
Hay; Squires, Burcher, Gibson, J.J. Williams; Bevan, Morgan; No. 8 Duggan (rep. Squire); T. Evans (Capt.), Keane, Martin, Neary; Orr, Windsor, Cotton (rep. C. Williams)
Tries: Squires (2), Orr, Gibson
Penalties: Gibson (2)

New Zealand Maoris
J. Whiu; G. Skipper, E. Stokes, D. Haynes; B. Osborne, E. Dunn; S. Going; M. West (rep. P. Quinn); T. Carter, V. Stewart, R. Lockwood, T. Waaka; L. Toki, T. Norton (Capt.), B. Bush
Tries: Going (2), Osborne
Conversions: Whiu (2)
Penalty: Whiu

Referee: J. Pring (Auckland)

Match 18:   British Isles *v*. Waikato
Hamilton, 16 July
British Isles 18   Waikato 13

British Isles
Irvine; Rees, McGeechan, Burcher, G. Evans; Bennett (Capt.), B. Williams (rep. Morgan); No. 8 Quinnell; Cobner, Brown, Beaumont, Squire; C. Williams (rep. Orr), Wheeler, Windsor
Tries: Rees (2), Irvine
Penalties: Bennett (2)

Waikato
T. Irwin; A. Clarke, K. Fawcett, J. O'Rourke; L. Hohaia, R. McGlashan; K. Greene (Capt.); D. Myers; P. Anderson, J. Sisley, R. Lockwood, I. Lockie; G. Irwin, P. Bernett, D. Olsen

Tries: Irwin, Lockwood
Penalty: Irwin
Conversion: Irwin

Referee: B. Dawson (Southland)

Match 19: British Isles *v.* New Zealand Juniors
Wellington, 20 July
British Isles 19   New Zealand Juniors 9

British Isles
Hay; G. Evans, McGeechan, Gibson (rep. J.J. Williams), Rees;
Bevan, Morgan; No. 8 Squire; Neary, Martin, Keane, T. Evans
(Capt.); Orr, Windsor, Cotton
Tries: Rees, Windsor, Squire
Conversions: Morgan (2)
Penalty: Morgan

New Zealand Juniors
B. Wilson; M. Watts, D. Fouhy, D. Haynes; S. Pokere, M. Sisam
(Capt.); M. Donaldson; G. Elvin; J. Sullivan (rep. A. Dawson), W.
Graham, B. Graig, G. Rich; M. Pervan, G. Collins, R. Ketels
Try: Pokere
Conversion: Wilson
Penalty: Wilson

Referee: M. Farnworth (Auckland)

Match 20: British Isles *v.* Auckland
Auckland, 23 July
British Isles 34   Auckland 15

British Isles
Irvine; J.J. Williams, Burcher, Fenwick, G. Evans; Bennett (Capt.),
Morgan; No. 8 Duggan; Quinnell, Brown, Beaumont, Neary; Cotton,
Wheeler, Price
Tries: Irvine (2), J.J. Williams, Duggan, Bennett
Conversion: Morgan
Penalties: Morgan (4)

Auckland
C. Farrell; B. Williams, T. Twigden; T. Morrison; P. Parlane, M.
Richards; B. Gemmell; G. Rich; D. Thorn, A. Haden, B. Munro, B.
Ashworth; B. Johnstone (Capt.), B. Hathaway, S. Watt (rep. G.
Denholm)
Try: Williams
Conversion: Parlane

Penalties: Williams, Watt (2)

Referee: D. Millar (Otago)

Match 21:   British Isles *v*. New Zealand (Third Test)
Dunedin, 31 July
British Isles 7   New Zealand 19

British Isles
Irvine; J.J. Williams (rep. McGeechan), Burcher, Fenwick, G. Evans; Bennett (Capt.), B. Williams (rep. Morgan); No. 8 Duggan; Quinnell, Brown, Beaumont, Cobner; Cotton, Wheeler, Price
Try: Duggan
Penalty: Irvine

New Zealand
B. Wilson; B. Ford, B. Robertson, B. Williams; B. Osborne, D. Bruce; L. Davis; L. Knight; I. Kirkpatrick, A. Haden, F. Oliver, G. Mourie; J. McEldowney, T. Norton (Capt.), B. Bush
Tries: Kirkpatrick, Haden
Conversion: Wilson
Penalties: Wilson (2)
Drop goal: Robertson

Referee: D. Millar (Otago)

Match 22:   British Isles *v*. Counties–Thames Valley
Pukekohe, 3 August
British Isles 35   Counties–Thames Valley 10

British Isles
Hay; G. Evans, Burcher, Gibson, Rees; Bevan, Morgan; No. 8 Squire; Neary (Capt.), Keane, Martin, T. Evans; Faulkner, Windsor, Price
Tries: Hay (2), G. Evans (2), Morgan.
Conversions: Morgan (3)
Penalties: Morgan (3)

Counties–Thames Valley
B. Lendrum; D. McMillan, B. Robertson, B. Milner; B. Duggan, G. Taylor; M. Codlin.(rep. T. Sheehan); A. Dawson; H. Harbraken, R. Craig, J. Rawiri, P. Clotworthy; J. Spiers, A. Dalton (Capt.), J. Hughes
Tries: McMillan, Lendrum
Conversion: Lendrum

Referee: P. McDavitt (Wellington)

Match 23:   British Isles *v*. North Auckland
Whangarei, 6 August
British Isles 18   North Auckland 7

British Isles
Irvine; G. Evans, McGeechan, Fenwick, Rees; Bennett (Capt.),
Lewis; No. 8 Duggan; Quinnell, Brown, Beaumont, Cobner (rep.
Neary); Orr, Wheeler, Cotton
Try: McGeechan
Conversion: Bennett
Penalties: Bennett (4)

North Auckland
M. Gunson; L. Roberts, C. Going, D. Haynes; J. Morgan, E. Dunn;
S. Going (Capt.); H. Sowman; T. Waaka, B. Holmes, H. Macdonald,
I. Phillips; W. Neville, P. Sloane, C. D'Arcy
Try: Haynes
Penalty: Gunson

Referee: J. Walker (Otago)

Match 24:   British Isles *v*. Bay of Plenty
Rotorua, 9 August
British Isles 23   Bay of Plenty 16

British Isles
Hay (rep. Irvine); Rees, Burcher, Gibson (rep. McGeechan), Bennett
(Capt.); Bevan, Lewis; No. 8 Duggan; T. Evans, Keane, Brown,
Squire; Faulkner, Windsor, Price
Tries: Rees, Burcher
Penalties: Bennett (5)

Bay of Plenty
G. Rowlands (Capt.); G. Moore, E. Stokes, J. Kamizona (rep. T.
Compton); M. Taylor (rep. R. Moon), J. Brake; T. Davis; M. Connor;
A. McNaughton, B. Spry, B. Jones, D. Matuschka; B. Keepa, R.
Doughty, J. Helmbright
Try: Taylor
Penalties: Rowlands (3)
Drop goal: Brake

Referee: N. Thomas (Manawatu)

Match 25:   British Isles *v*. New Zealand (Fourth Test)
Auckland, 13 August
British Isles 9   New Zealand 11

British Isles
Irvine; Rees, McGeechan, Fenwick, G. Evans; Bennett (Capt.), Morgan; No. 8 Duggan; Squire, Brown, Beaumont, Neary; Cotton, Wheeler, Price
Try: Morgan
Conversion: Morgan
Penalty: Morgan

New Zealand
B. Wilson; B. Williams, B. Robertson, B. Ford (rep. M. Taylor); B. Osborne, D. Bruce; L. Davis; L. Knight; G. Mourie, A. Haden, F. Oliver, I. Kirkpatrick; K. Lambert, T. Norton (Capt.), J. McEldowney (rep. B. Bush)
Try: Knight
Penalties: Wilson (2)

Referee: D. Millar (Otago)

Playing record in New Zealand

Played 25: won 21; drawn 0; lost 4
Points: for 586; against 295
Tries: for 80; against 29
Conversions: for 40; against 13
Penalties: for 62; against 46
Drop goals: for 0; against 5

Match 26:   British Isles *v.* **Fiji**
Suva, 16 August
British Isles 21   Fiji 25

British Isles
Irvine; G. Evans, McGeechan, Burcher, Bennett (Capt.); Bevan, Lewis; No. 8 Squire; T. Evans (rep. Brown), Martin, Beaumont, Neary; Faulkner, Windsor, Price
Tries: Bennett, Beaumont, Burcher
Conversions: Bennett (3)
Penalty: Bennett

Fiji
K. Musunamasi; J. Kuinikoro, Q. Ratu, S. Nasave, W. Gavidi; P. Tikoisuva (Capt.), S. Viriviri; No. 8 V. Ratudradra; V. Narasia, I. Taoba, I. Tuisese, R. Qariniqio; J. Rauto, A. Racika, N. Ratudina
Tries: Narasia (2), Kuinikoro, Racika, Rauto
Conversion: Racika
Drop goal: Tikoisuva

Referee: S. Koroi

The players

The tour party

	Date of birth	Height ft in.	Weight st. lb.	Club
Full backs				
Andy Irvine (Scotland)	16. 9.1951	5 10	12 8	Heriot's FP
Bruce Hay (Scotland)	23. 5.1950	5 10	13 5	Boroughmuir
Wings				
Elgan Rees (Wales)	5. 1.1954	5 8	12 7	Neath
Peter Squires (England)	4. 8.1951	5 9	11 7	Harrogate
John Williams (Wales)	1. 4.1948	5 9	11 7	Llanelli
Gareth Evans (Wales)	2.11.1953	5 11	13 11	Newport
Centres				
Mike Gibson (Ireland)	3.12.1942	5 11	12 7	North of Ireland
Steve Fenwick (Wales)	23. 7.1951	5 10	13 2	Bridgend
David Burcher (Wales)	26.10.1951	5 10	13 5	Newport
Ian McGeechan (Scotland)	30.10.1946	5 9	11 3	Headingley
Fly halves				
John Bevan (Wales)	12. 3.1948	5 8	12 8	Aberavon
Phil Bennett, Capt. (Wales)	24.10.1948	5 7	11 4	Llanelli
Scrum halves				
Doug Morgan (Scotland)	9. 3.1947	5 9	11 10	Stewart's Melville FP
Brynmor Williams (Wales)	29.10.1951	5 9	12 7	Cardiff
*Alun Lewis (Wales)	15. 1.1956	5 10	13 4	London Welsh
No. 8s				
Willie Duggan (Ireland)	12. 3.1950	6 3	15 12	Blackrock College
*Jeff Squire (Wales)	23. 9.1951	6 3	16 0	Newport

	Date of birth	Height ft in.	Weight st. lb.	Club
Flankers				
Tony Neary (England)	25.11.1948	6 1	14 7	Broughton Park
Trevor Evans (Wales)	26.11.1947	6 1	14 4	Swansea
Derek Quinnell (Wales)	22. 5.1949	6 3	16 7	Llanelli
Terry Cobner (Wales)	10. 1.1946	6 0	14 4	Pontypool
Locks				
Gordon Brown (Scotland)	1.11.1946	6 5	16 12	West of Scotland
Nigel Horton (England)	13. 4.1948	6 5	16 8	Moseley
Moss Keane (Ireland)	27. 7.1948	6 4½	16 13	Landsdown
Allan Martin (Wales)	11.12.1948	6 5	16 8	Aberavon
*Billy Beaumont (England)	9. 3.1952	6 3	16 0	Fylde
Props				
Fran Cotton (England)	3. 1.1948	6 2	16 7	Sale
Phil Orr (Ireland)	14.12.1950	5 11	15 7	Old Wesley
Graham Price (Wales)	24. 1.1951	6 0	15 4	Pontypool
Clive Williams (Wales)	2.11.1951	6 0	15 8	Aberavon
*Charlie Faulkner (Wales)	27. 2.1944	5 10	15 12	Pontypool
Hookers				
Peter Wheeler (England)	26.11.1948	5 11	14 0	Leicester
Bobby Windsor (Wales)	31. 1.1948	5 9	14 9	Pontypool

*indicates players joining the party during the tour.

Their appearances

	Test appearances	Total appearances	Tries	Conversions	Penalties	Points
Full backs						
Andy Irvine	4	18	11	8	9	87
Bruce Hay	-	11	5	-	-	20
Wings						
Elgan Rees	1	12	8	-	-	32
Peter Squires	1	9	5	-	-	20
John Williams	3	14	10	-	-	40
Gareth Evans	3	17	6	-	-	24
Centres						
Mike Gibson	-	11	2	2	4	24
Steve Fenwick	4	12	1	1	3	15
David Burcher	1	14	4	-	-	16
Ian McGeechan	4	15	3	-	-	12

	Test appearances	Total appearances	Tries	Conversions	Penalties	Points
Fly halves						
John Bevan	-	11	1	-	-	4
Phil Bennett, Capt.	4	14	2	13	26	112
Scrum halves						
Doug Morgan	2	15	3	16	18	98
Brynmor Williams	3	12	3	-	-	12
Alun Lewis	-	2	-	-	-	-
No. 8s						
Willie Duggan	4	16	2	-	-	8
Jeff Squire	1	14	3	-	-	12
Flankers						
Tony Neary	1	13	-	-	-	-
Trevor Evans	1	13	-	-	-	-
Derek Quinnell	2	13	2	-	-	8
Terry Cobner	3	11	3	-	-	12
Locks						
Gordon Brown	3	14	1	-	-	4
Nigel Horton	-	4	-	-	-	-
Moss Keane	1	12	1	-	-	4
Allan Martin	1	13	-	-	2	6
Billy Beaumont	3	9	-	-	-	-
Props						
Fran Cotton	3	16	-	-	-	-
Phil Orr	1	12	1	-	-	4
Graham Price	4	14	-	-	-	-
Clive Williams	-	9	1	-	-	4
Charlie Faulkner	-	2	-	-	-	-
Hookers						
Peter Wheeler	3	13	1	-	-	4
Bobby Windsor	1	13	1	-	-	4
Total						
for			80	40	62	586
against			29	13	46 (and 5 drop goals)	295

Index

Main references are in **bold type**